CGP has Year 8 English totally covered!

KS3 English can feel tricky at times, but this handy CGP Workbook
will take you through everything you need to know, topic by topic.

Each section starts with a warm-up to get you in the groove, followed by heaps of
practice questions to help you master all those pesky KS3 reading and writing skills.

Once you've got the hang of each section, you can bring all your knowledge together
in the review sections. You'll also find answers to every question at the back. Enjoy!

CGP — still the best! ☺

Our sole aim here at CGP is to produce the highest quality books —
carefully written, immaculately presented and dangerously close to being funny.

Then we work our socks off to get them out to you
— at the cheapest possible prices.

Contents

How To Use This Book 1

Section 1: Reading — Audience and Purpose
Before you Start 3
Different Types of Text 4
Audience 5
Purpose 6
Context 7

Section 2: Reading — Non-Fiction Texts
Before you Start 8
Finding Evidence in the Text 9
Summarising 10
Working Out What's Going On 11
Layout and Structure 12
Language Techniques 13
Tone 15
What You Think 16
The Author's Intentions 17

Section 3: Reading — Fiction and Plays
Before you Start 18
Finding Evidence in the Text 19
Summarising 20
Working Out What's Going On 21
Structure 22
Themes 23
Language Techniques 24
Understanding the Characters 25
Understanding the Setting 27
Interpreting Plays 29
Staging and Performance 31
What You Think 32

Section 4: Reading — Poetry
Before you Start 33
Working Out What's Going On 34
Structure 35
Themes 36
Voice 37
Techniques 38

Section 5: Reading — Comparing Texts
Before you Start 39
Comparing Texts 40

Contents

Section 6: Reading Review
Animal Farm by George Orwell...44
Face by Benjamin Zephaniah..46
Someone, No one: A Flight of Fantasy...48
Romeo and Juliet by William Shakespeare..50

Section 7: Writing — Non-Fiction Writing
Before you Start..52
Planning...53
Structure..54
Quoting...56
Writing Essays...57
Formal and Informal Language..58
Writing to Inform, Explain and Advise...59
Writing to Persuade and Argue..61

Section 8: Writing — Fiction Writing
Before you Start..63
Planning...64
Structure..65
Building Character..66
Building Setting...67
Writing Stories..68
Writing Scripts..69
Poetry...70

Section 9: Writing — Writing Properly
Before you Start..71
Punctuation Mix..72
Structuring Your Writing..73
Redrafting and Proofreading..74

Section 10: Writing — Making It Interesting
Before you Start..75
Using Different Techniques..76
Figurative Language...77

Section 11: Writing Review
Writing Review..78

Answers..82

Published by CGP

Editors:
Emma Cleasby, Rachel Craig-McFeely, Becca Lakin, Katya Parkes, Hannah Roscoe, Rebecca Russell, Kirsty Sweetman

Acknowledgements:

Extract on page 21 © William Sutcliffe, 2017, We See Everything, Bloomsbury Publishing Plc.

Extract on page 24 © Martine Murray, 2003, How to Make a Bird. Sydney: Allen & Unwin.

Page 25: Extract from A Skinful of Shadows, first published in 2017 by Macmillan Children's Books, an imprint of Pan Macmillan. Reproduced by permission of Macmillan Publishers International Limited. Copyright © Frances Hardinge 2017.

Page 25: Material from RED LEAVES by Sita Brahmachari is reproduced by kind permission of the author. Published by Macmillan Children's Books.

Page 26: Extract from "Kes" © 2000 by Barry Hines and Lawrence Till reprinted with permission from Nick Hern Books: www.nickhernbooks.co.uk

Extract on page 27 is taken from Island Songs and is reproduced by kind permission of the author and the publishers, Allison and Busby Ltd. Copyright © 2005 by Alex Wheatle.

Page 29: OUR DAY OUT by WILLY RUSSELL by kind permission of Negus-Fancey Agents Ltd.

Extract on page 32: The Book Thief by Markus Zusak © 2016.
By arrangement with the licensor, Markus Zusak, c/- Curtis Brown (Aust) Pty Ltd.

Page 34: Poem "Water Picture" from Collected Poems, 2013, © May Swenson 1958.
Used with permission of The Literary Estate of May Swenson. All rights reserved.

Page 35: Poem "Russian Doll" is from The Language of Cat by Rachel Rooney. © Rachel Rooney 2011, published by Otter-Barry Books and reproduced with permission from David Higham Associates Ltd on behalf of Rachel Rooney.

Page 36: Poem "Everyone Sang" © Siegfried Sassoon by kind permission of the Estate of George Sassoon.

Page 36: Poem "They dropped like Flakes" is taken from THE POEMS OF EMILY DICKINSON, edited by Thomas H. Johnson, Cambridge, Mass.: The Belknap Press of Harvard University Press, Copyright © 1951, 1955 by the President and Fellows of Harvard College. Copyright © renewed 1979, 1983 by the President and Fellows of Harvard College. Copyright © 1914, 1918, 1919, 1924, 1929, 1930, 1932, 1935, 1937, 1942, by Martha Dickinson Bianchi. Copyright © 1952, 1957, 1958, 1963, 1965, by Mary L. Hampson. Used by permission. All rights reserved.

Poem "Right to Be" used on page 37 written by Amyra León. Used with permission.

Page 38: Poem "Taal" by Imtiaz Dharker from Over the Moon (Bloodaxe Books, 2016).
Reproduced with permission of Bloodaxe Books. www.bloodaxebooks.com

Extract on page 46 © Benjamin Zephaniah, 1999, Face, Bloomsbury Publishing Plc.

A note for teachers, parents and caregivers

Just something to bear in mind if you're choosing further reading for Year 8 pupils — all the extracts in this book are suitable for children of this age, but we can't vouch for the full texts they're taken from, or other works by the same authors.

ISBN: 978 1 78908 784 0

With thanks to Rose Jones and Matthew Sims for the proofreading.
With thanks to Jan Greenway for the copyright research.

Clipart from Corel®
Printed by Elanders Ltd, Newcastle upon Tyne.

Based on the classic CGP style created by Richard Parsons.

Text, design, layout and original illustrations © Coordination Group Publications Ltd. (CGP) 2021
All rights reserved.

Photocopying this book is not permitted, even if you have a CLA licence.
Extra copies are available from CGP with next day delivery • 0800 1712 712 • www.cgpbooks.co.uk

How To Use This Book

- Hold the book <u>upright</u>, approximately <u>50 cm</u> from your face, ensuring that the text looks like <u>this</u>, not सिर्फ. Alternatively, place the book on a <u>flat</u> surface (e.g. a table or desk) and sit in front of the book, at a comfortable distance that doesn't make the text too small to read.
- In case of emergency, press the two halves of the book together <u>firmly</u> in order to close.
- Before attempting to use this book, familiarise yourself with the following <u>safety information</u>:

Different schools cover different Key Stage 3 English topics at <u>different times</u>. <u>Don't panic</u> if you come across something you haven't learnt yet — just <u>skip</u> that topic and move on.

The book is split into two parts — <u>Reading</u> and <u>Writing</u>. In the Reading section, you'll be answering questions based on <u>texts</u>. In the Writing section, the questions will help you improve your <u>writing skills</u> and write some of <u>your own stuff</u>.

There are <u>eleven sections</u> covering different topics, so it's easy to find questions on the <u>specific thing</u> you want to practise.

Every question has an <u>answer</u> at the back of the book — the answers start on page 82.

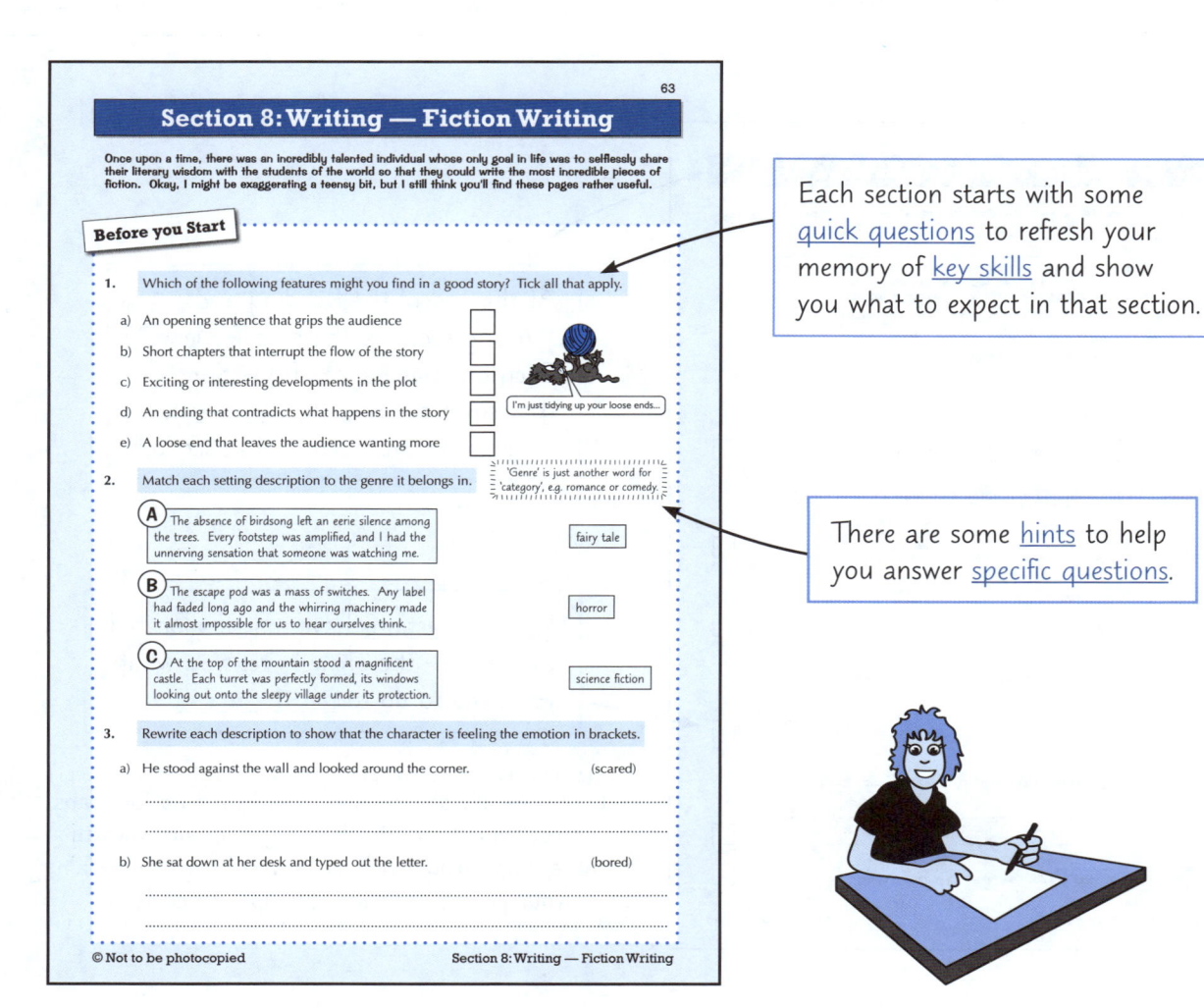

Each section starts with some <u>quick questions</u> to refresh your memory of <u>key skills</u> and show you what to expect in that section.

There are some <u>hints</u> to help you answer <u>specific questions</u>.

How To Use This Book

Each topic has a page or two of questions that get more challenging as you work through them.

Most questions have dotted lines where you can write your answers. For questions where you need to give a longer answer, you'll need a separate piece of paper.

Some pages have a Now Try This box at the bottom — these are extra tasks to give you even more practice.

At the end of the Reading and Writing sections, there's a Review. Each one has pages of questions that cover the reading and writing skills you've practised in that section.

Review questions have marks allocated to them — the answers tell you what you need to do to get the marks.

Look carefully at how many marks are up for grabs in each question. If a Reading question is worth more than a couple of marks, you'll need to explain your points, backing them up with evidence.

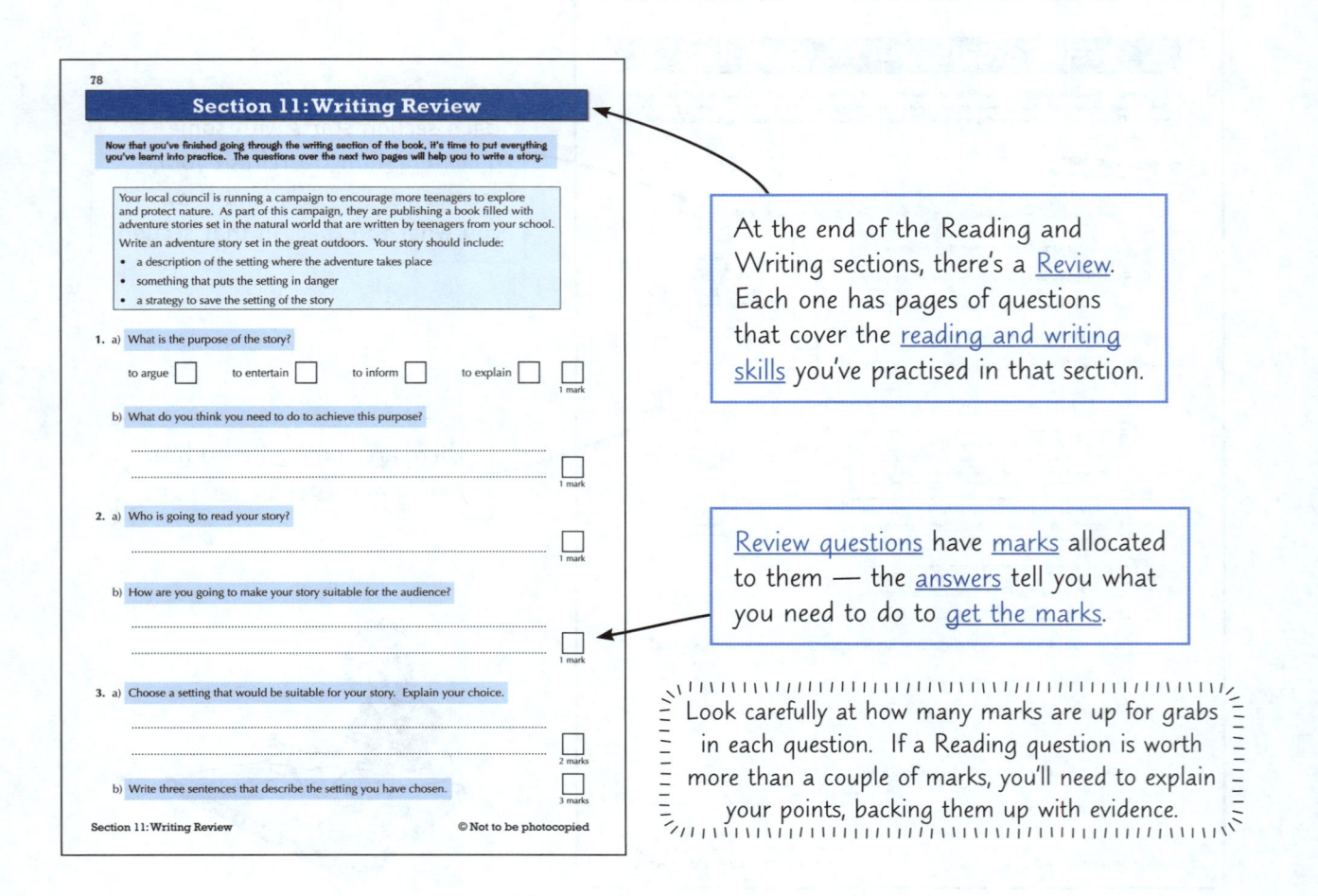

Section 1: Reading — Audience and Purpose

Every text you read has an audience and a purpose — for example, *you* are my audience, and my purpose is to *inform* you about the joys of English. The audience and purpose of a text affect how it's written.

Before you Start

1. a) Draw lines to match each type of text to its defining feature.

Fable	A story which is performed and has stage directions
Myth	A made-up story about gods or heroes
Play	A short story which has a moral

   b) What is the main purpose of the texts above? Tick one box.

   to argue ☐   to inform ☐   to entertain ☐   to explain ☐

2. Circle the most appropriate audience for each text below.

   Microchipping is by far the best way to ensure a lost pet can be reunited with its owner. The procedure is quick and simple, and will give you peace of mind.

   vets / pet owners

   Some people prefer to throw themselves in at the deep end, but I always recommend starting off with something small and less detailed. Get to grips with stitching and following a pattern before you contemplate working on anything complex.

   a beginner / an expert

3. Read texts A-C, then fill out the table to show their intended audience and purpose.

   A Sheep are sometimes called other names. Baby sheep are called 'lambs'. Mummy sheep are called 'ewes'.

   B If you're looking for a fun but low-cost day out, I would suggest taking your family to a local beach — your children will love it.

   C Do you want a break from homework? Do you like having fun? If you've answered 'yes' to these questions, join netball club!

Text	Audience	Purpose
A		
B		
C		

© Not to be photocopied

Different Types of Texts

There are loads of types of text — poems, articles, instructions, novels... and that's just a handful of examples. You need to know that different texts have different features, and how those features affect the reader.

1. a) What type of text do you think each extract below is from?

> **A** Leaves contain chlorophyll, a pigment which absorbs sunlight. This allows them to undertake a process called photosynthesis, in which sunlight, water and carbon dioxide from the air are combined to produce energy for the plant.

> **B** To achieve the highest-quality finish, it is advised that application of this paint should not be attempted until the plaster is fully set. To apply the paint evenly, use long, sweeping strokes of the arm and apply at least two coats.

   i) ....   ii) ....

b) Explain why you chose your answers in part a).

2. The extract below is about representation in children's books.

> I'm speaking to you today because I believe that it is vitally important that children feel represented by characters in fiction: these characters are their heroes and role models. Yet people of colour remain significantly under-represented in children's books today. Although representation has gradually increased, a recent study showed that only a small minority of children's books feature characters of colour. So let me ask you: do you think this is acceptable? Surely not. The situation for creators of colour is even more concerning, as less than a tenth of authors and illustrators are from a minority ethnic background.

a) What type of text is this from? ....

b) Explain briefly why you chose your answer to part a).

....

....

c) Write 'Fact' or 'Opinion' to show whether the quotes below are facts or opinions.

   i) 'it is vitally important that children feel represented'   ....

   ii) 'representation has gradually increased'   ....

   iii) 'The situation for creators of colour is even more concerning'   ....

d) Give one fact from the text that isn't mentioned in part c).

....

....

Section 1: Reading — Audience and Purpose

Audience

The audience of a text can affect its style, content and presentation — you wouldn't speak in the same way to a toddler and your teacher. You can use clues (e.g. vocabulary) to work out who a text's audience is.

1. Label each text with its intended audience from the box. Watch out, there will be some left over.

   | newspaper readers   teachers   toddlers   expert historians   friends |

   a) Based on this evidence, we must reconsider the impact of the Beaker people on the early Bronze Age.

   ....

   b) Today we learnt about the Bronze Age and Mrs Pip let us look at some artefacts — it was awesome!

   ....

   c) Last week, contractors at a building site in Wales accidentally uncovered a rare Bronze Age burial site.

   ....

2. Below are two recipes for making a cake.

   A Sift the flour into the wet ingredients, stirring together to combine. Once the mixture reaches the desired consistency, pour it into the pre-prepared tins and bake at 180 °C until golden brown.

   B Using a sieve, shake the flour into the bowl which contains the melted butter, chocolate and eggs. Next, carefully stir the mixture with a spoon until all the flour is combined.

   a) Circle the text that would be most suitable for an adult with no baking experience.

   b) Explain why the text you circled is the most suitable for this audience.

   ....
   ....

   c) Who do you think is the intended audience of the other text? Explain why the text would suit that audience.

   ....
   ....
   ....

   d) Rewrite Text B to make it suitable for young children.

NOW TRY THIS — Now it's time to apply your knowledge about audience to your writing. Write a paragraph for your teacher describing your greatest strength. Then, rewrite the paragraph so that it's aimed at your friends. Think carefully about the vocabulary and style you use in each paragraph.

© Not to be photocopied   Section 1: Reading — Audience and Purpose

Purpose

My purpose in life is to toil endlessly, producing books to educate people — I know, I'm pretty selfless. Texts also have a purpose — most are written to either entertain, inform, explain, advise, argue or persuade.

1. a) Match each extract to its purpose by writing A-D in the boxes.

A) You could take up knitting, as it is both a relaxing and productive hobby.	B) She snarled, her bared teeth glinting like hundreds of tiny white daggers.	C) The use of fossil fuels must be banned, or else our planet will face total devastation.	D) Bouldering is one of the most common forms of climbing.

    to entertain ☐   to argue ☐   to inform ☐   to advise ☐

    b) For each extract above, explain how you can tell what its purpose is.

2. The extract below is from a letter.

    > I am writing with regard to my recent experience at your café. Firstly, your customer service was abominable. The waitress ignored my table for twenty minutes, before proceeding to chew gum whilst taking our order. Secondly, the food was repulsive: my soup was slimy and ice-cold.

    a) What is the purpose of this text? Tick a box.

    to inform ☐   to complain ☐   to entertain ☐   to argue ☐   to explain ☐

    b) Explain how the text is suited to its purpose.

    ....

    ....

3. The extract below is from an article that is meant to advise someone, but its style doesn't fit its purpose.

    > 1. *Escape to Albion* is a fantasy novel about King Arthur, who has been reincarnated in the modern age. It contains comedy, drama and romance and has won several awards.
    > 2. *Kiki and the Castle* is a short story about a young girl who discovers an ancient castle.

    a) Explain how the text could be adapted to fit its purpose better.

    ....

    ....

    b) Rewrite the text so that it suits its purpose.

Section 1: Reading — Audience and Purpose

Context

Context is information about the text's background, such as when and where it was written. Just like audience and purpose, context can affect style and content — so knowing a text's context is pretty useful.

1. The extract below is adapted from *Great Expectations* by Charles Dickens, which was written in the Victorian period. Pip (the narrator), a blacksmith's apprentice, has recently become extremely wealthy.

   > "Mr. Trabb," said I, "it's an unpleasant thing to have to mention, because it looks like boasting; but I have come into a great deal of money."
   > A change passed over Mr. Trabb.
   > "My dear sir," said Mr. Trabb, as he respectfully bent his body, opened his arms, and took the liberty of touching me on each elbow, "Would you do me the favour of stepping into the shop?"

   a) i) How does Mr Trabb speak to Pip when he finds out that Pip is wealthy?

   ....

   ....

   ii) What does this suggest about attitudes towards wealth in Charles Dickens's time?

2. The poem below is *Sonnet 9: On Returning to the Front after Leave* by Alan Seeger. It describes Seeger's experience as a soldier in World War One.

   > Apart sweet women (for whom Heaven be blessed),
   > Comrades, you cannot think how thin and blue
   > Look the leftovers of mankind that rest,
   > Now that the cream has been skimmed off in you.
   > War has its horrors, but has this of good —
   > That its sure processes sort out and bind
   > Brave hearts in one intrepid brotherhood
   > And leave the shams and imbeciles behind.
   > Now turn we joyful to the great attacks,
   > Not only that we face in a fair field
   > Our valiant foe and all his deadly tools,
   > But also that we turn disdainful backs
   > On that poor world we scorn yet die to shield —
   > That world of cowards, hypocrites, and fools.

   a) Write down a phrase that shows that the narrator acknowledges the negative side of war.

   ....

   b) Give one good thing that the narrator believes can come from war.

   ....

   c) What impression do you get of the narrator's attitude towards soldiers in World War One? Explain your answer using details from the text.

Section 2: Reading — Non-Fiction Texts

Non-fiction texts are everywhere, from newspapers, to adverts, to postcards. They're written with a particular purpose in mind, e.g. to inform or persuade, and writers will include certain features to help achieve that purpose. Have a go at the questions below to get to grips with reading non-fiction texts.

Before you Start

1. The extract below is from a newspaper article.

   > **SHARK SPOTTED NEAR POPULAR SEASIDE RESORT**
   >
   > Weekend holidaymakers were stunned to discover a shark swimming just offshore from a popular beach. Spotted by a group of surfers, the shark remained in the area for several hours before retreating to deeper water.
   >
   > According to Coral Fischer, head of a local marine wildlife charity, it's not uncommon to see sharks in these waters. "People were understandably perplexed to see one in this particular area, but it's actually more common than they realise. The UK is regularly visited by many different species of shark, and some of them are here year-round."
   >
   > While the shark poses very little threat to beach-goers, the coastguard is urging everyone to keep their distance. Fischer welcomes this, adding, "It's really important to give these creatures space — they're easily disturbed by human activity, and we must be mindful of that."

   a) What is the purpose of the article's introduction? Give evidence to support your answer.

   ....

   ....

   b) How does Coral Fischer feel about the coastguard's advice?
   What evidence is there in the text?

   ....

   ....

   c) i) How does the article make you feel about sharks?

   ....

   ii) Explain why the article makes you feel this way.

   ....

   ....

   d) Write a short summary of the article in your own words.

Finding Evidence in the Text

There are different ways to support the points you make — maybe a short example, a nice little quote or perhaps a general impression. However you do it, make sure you back up your answers using the text.

1. The extract below is from an article about the Moon landing in 1969.

> In 1961, President John F. Kennedy announced his intention to send astronauts to the Moon and return them to Earth. It was an ambitious project that would take eight years of careful preparation to realise. Sadly, Kennedy wouldn't be alive to see it.
>
> In July 1969, astronauts Neil Armstrong, Buzz Aldrin and Michael Collins lifted off from the Kennedy Space Center, Florida, hoping to make history as the first humans to land on the lunar surface. It would take three days for them to travel the hundreds of thousands of miles separating the Earth and the Moon. On 20th July, Armstrong and Aldrin boarded the Eagle (the descent spacecraft), leaving Collins to pilot the command module and prepare for their return. It was a tense wait for Mission Control as Armstrong and Aldrin began their slow descent to the surface. But after thirteen long minutes, the control room could finally celebrate as Armstrong declared that the Eagle had landed safely.
>
> Millions of people watched the Moon landing live, and it remains a pivotal moment in human history. It paved the way for five subsequent manned missions, the last of which was in 1972. NASA has announced plans to send more astronauts to the Moon by 2024, which will help them to prepare for manned missions to Mars.

a) Complete the table by answering the questions.

How long did it take to prepare for the Moon landing?	
Where did the astronauts begin their journey?	
How many more times has NASA sent people to the Moon?	
When is NASA planning to send more astronauts to the Moon?	

b) How can you tell that the descent to the Moon was a dangerous undertaking?

....

....

c) How can you tell that the Moon landing captured the public's imagination?

....

d) Write out the part of the text that tells you how important the Moon landing was.

....

Summarising

Allow me to summarise why writing summaries is a really useful skill — they let you condense the key ideas in a text into a much more manageable chunk and they get rid of any information that is irrelevant.

1. The extracts below are from reviews of the same film by two different authors.

   A When I first heard who had been cast in the film, I had high hopes of it being another one of Sherman Jolt's cinematic masterpieces. The star-studded line-up boasts multiple awards, but I found the acting to be average at best. The characters were highly predictable and a burden on the terribly uninventive plot.

   B Fans of Jolt's early work will recognise the signature suspense and high-octane action in his newest film. Set in the distant future, an unlikely group of people is brought together to solve a mystery that threatens life as they know it. The story is bursting with exciting twists and revelations that kept me on the edge of my seat.

   a) i) Tick the option that best describes how Author A feels about the film.

   excited ☐   disgusted ☐   impressed ☐   disappointed ☐

   ii) Tick the option that best describes how Author B feels about the film.

   terrified ☐   gripped ☐   bored ☐   confused ☐

   b) Explain your answers to part a) by writing a brief summary of each author's opinion.

2. The extract below is from a speech about public transport.

   The state of public transport in this country is absolutely unacceptable. Not only are trains frequently delayed or cancelled, but they are outrageously overpriced. There is an almost complete absence of buses in rural locations, and in the few areas where service is provided, it is patchy and unreliable at best. This lack of public transport forces people to travel by car and thereby contribute to the shocking levels of pollution and congestion on our roads.

   a) i) Summarise the tone of the extract above.

   ....

   ii) Explain your answer to part i) by writing a summary of the extract.

   b) i) Suggest an appropriate title for the extract. Make sure it reflects the extract's content.

   ....

   ii) Explain why you have chosen this title. Refer to the extract in your answer.

Section 2: Reading — Non-Fiction Texts

Working Out What's Going On

Sometimes the details in a text will be immediately obvious, but this won't always be the case. You also need to be able to infer information by reading between the lines so you can draw your own conclusions.

1. The extract below is from an information leaflet about titanosaurs.

    > The largest dinosaurs to walk the planet belonged to a group called sauropods. Instantly recognisable by their long necks and tails, these four-legged, herbivorous giants include iconic species like Brachiosaurus. Thought to be around 20 metres from head to tail, the Brachiosaurus was once considered the giant of the dinosaur world. However, more recently discovered fossils have brought to light the existence of even bigger dinosaurs. These super-sized browsers — appropriately dubbed 'titanosaurs' — dwarfed their sauropod cousins by a considerable margin, and currently hold the title of largest land animals to ever exist.
    >
    > The largest known species of titanosaur, Argentinosaurus and Patagotitan, are estimated to have reached up to 40 metres in length. However, this figure is still debated by palaeontologists. At present, no complete skeletons have been unearthed and therefore, predictions have had to be based on expertise alongside incomplete evidence. Regardless, making these predictions is an astonishing achievement and, as research and technology advance, more precise predictions, or perhaps even new discoveries, may be made.

    a) How did titanosaurs get their name?

    ....

    b) Why was the discovery of titanosaurs so remarkable?

    ....

    ....

    c) Are the palaeontologists' predictions likely to be completely accurate? Explain your answer.

    ....

    ....

    d) i) How do you think the author feels about the discovery of titanosaurs?

    ....

    ii) How can you tell that the author feels this way?
    Use details from the extract to explain your answer.

    e) Do you think some dinosaurs existed that were even larger than titanosaurs?
    Explain your answer using evidence from the extract.

Layout and Structure

A text's purpose shapes its presentation. Writers often use the layout of a text to create specific effects for the reader. Pay close attention to a text's structure too — how the information is ordered can be very important.

1. The extract below is from an advert for a holiday park.

   > **Looking for an AFFORDABLE summer getaway?**
   > **Choose ELMSMERE HOLIDAY PARK!**
   >
   > For a limited time only, we're HALVING the price of our lakeside cabins.
   > Rates start from as little as £200 per adult and all children under 10 go FREE!
   > Treat your family to the holiday they deserve at a fraction of the usual price.
   >
   > - Unique, tranquil setting
   > - Pet friendly
   > - On-site entertainment facilities
   > - Unbeatable value for money
   >
   > **Book NOW to take advantage of this LIMITED-TIME OFFER!**

   a) Tick the option which best describes the purpose of the bullet points in the advert.

   | to give details about the offer ☐ | to summarise what the park has to offer ☐ | to make the advert look more interesting ☐ |

   b) Some words in the advert are written in upper case.
   Why do you think this has been done? Explain your answer.

   ....

   ....

   c) Do you think the first two lines of the advert are an effective introduction?
   Give two reasons for your answer.

   d) Why do you think the author chose to end the advert with the final sentence?

2. Read the recipe below. Explain why the layout isn't appropriate for this text type, then explain how you could change the layout to improve it.

   > Crush the garlic, then roughly chop the onion and bacon. Gently fry everything on a medium heat, being careful not to burn the garlic as this will add a bitter taste to the dish. Once the spaghetti is cooked, remove it from the water and add it to the other pan. Don't get rid of the pasta water as you may need it to loosen the sauce. Lightly beat the egg and stir in the grated Parmesan cheese. Season with a pinch of black pepper, but don't add any salt — the cheese will provide this. Pour the mixture onto the spaghetti and stir well to ensure everything is fully coated. The dish is ready when the egg is cooked and the cheese has completely melted. Finish with a generous serving of Parmesan.

   This is acceptable.

Language Techniques

The purpose of a text can also affect the language techniques that writers use. Different techniques can affect the reader in a number of ways. You need to be able to identify these techniques and explain their impact.

1. The extract below is from a speech.

   > I am truly humbled to be presented with such a prestigious prize. When I started this venture, I doubted whether it would ever be successful. In the first few years, progress was a million times slower than you could possibly imagine, and I suspect most people would, understandably, have admitted defeat. But those early struggles are the reason why I am standing here now — they drove me to keep going no matter what. As my late father used to say, life is a road paved with opportunities, and it is up to you to make the most of them.

   a) Write the name of each language technique next to the examples from the text.

   | presented with such a prestigious prize | → | .... |

   | progress was a million times slower than you could possibly imagine | → | .... |

   | life is a road paved with opportunities | → | .... |

   b) Why do you think the author used these techniques in their speech? Explain your answer.

   ....

   ....

   ....

2. The extract below is from a travel guide to Egypt.

   > The Valley of the Kings is one of the most iconic Ancient Egyptian sites still in existence. What may just look like a sandy ruin from the outside is actually a window into one of history's most fascinating and enduring civilisations. A total of 63 tombs have been unearthed here, although experts believe that the valley may still be concealing some of its deepest secrets from them.
   >   Many of the tombs showcase stunning statues, carvings and sarcophagi. But be warned — the guards are like hawks, and will swoop in on anyone taking photos without permission.

   a) Write out two examples of descriptive language from the extract.

   ....

   ....

   b) Why has the writer included descriptive language in this type of text?

Language Techniques

3.   Extracts A-C are from different types of text.

A Although I was sceptical about the candle's 'Autumn Leaves' scent, I found the aroma extremely pleasant. The deep, earthy, warming tones conjure up peaceful memories of strolling through a forest on an autumn day — the warming glow of sunshine on your face, the soft crunch of dry leaves underfoot... If you're after a scent that really delights and transports, I would highly recommend this lovely candle.

B Tired of tuna mayo? Cheesed off with cheddar? Feeling hate for ham? Add some punch to your lunch with McSarnie's Crazy Combo Cards! Just pick two cards at random from the deck and voilà — that's your sandwich filling. With thousands of possible combinations, it's out with the old, bland offerings and in with new, exciting flavours. Peanut butter and egg — why not? Jam and roast chicken — you bet! Break away from the norm and see where McSarnie's can take you.

C This breakthrough is truly astonishing: it's as if we've been living in a dark room our whole lives and someone's suddenly opened the curtains. The thrilling discovery is sure to revolutionise the world of science and technology — we will feel its impact on our lives for years to come.

a)   i)   Extracts A and B both use persuasive language. For each extract, name a persuasive language technique which has been used and write down an example from the text.

....

....

ii)   What effect do each of these techniques have on the reader?

iii) Why do you think the authors of extracts A and B have used persuasive language? Explain your answer, referring to the purpose of each of the extracts.

b)   i)   Write down one example of emotive language used in Extract C.

Emotive language is language that prompts an emotional response from the reader.

....

ii)   Why do you think the author has chosen to use emotive language in this text?

....

....

....

NOW TRY THIS Using Extract B as a guide, write an advert for the candle mentioned in Extract A. Think about the purpose of the text and which language techniques would work best. Try to include at least three different techniques from the past few pages, and be as creative and inventive as you can.

Tone

A text's tone is how it sounds when you read it. It could be angry and critical, or maybe chatty and friendly. In any case, you need to be able to explain why a text has a certain tone and the impact this has on the reader.

1. The extract below is from an email.

   > It was lovely to hear from you — it feels like an eternity since we last saw each other. I'm glad to hear that everyone is OK and keeping busy. We have a lot to be getting on with. Tim's still struggling to find a job so he's helped out a bit. He's got a few interviews next week though so fingers crossed... Meanwhile I'm trying to unpack all the boxes from the house move — there's just so much stuff and nowhere to put it!

   a) i) Tick the option which best describes the tone of the extract.

   overwhelmed ☐   regretful ☐   excited ☐   frustrated ☐

   ii) Explain why you've ticked that option.

   ....

   ....

   b) Write down one word to describe the tone you'd expect the types of text below to have.

   i) a letter to the head of a company   ....

   ii) an article offering advice about knitting   ....

   iii) a postcard from your best friend   ....

2. Text A is a note to the author's best friend and Text B is from a flyer produced by a local pub.

   A I regret to inform you that I am no longer able to attend your birthday party. I apologise if this causes you any inconvenience.

   B We're really pleased to announce that after months of refurbishment, the pub will be reopening this Saturday. Join us for a glass of bubbly and karaoke from 7 pm.

   a) Briefly describe the tone of each of the texts.

   ....

   ....

   b) Do you think the tone of each text is appropriate for its purpose? Explain your answer.

What You Think

You've now looked at lots of ways that writers can affect their readers. So I think it's time for you to use that brilliant noggin of yours to form your own opinions and conclusions about a text. Oh how I spoil you.

1. The extract below is from a school newspaper.

> School uniform has always been a contentious issue. This week, our newspaper carried out a short survey with our fellow students and teachers to find out how we all feel about our uniform and whether anything needs to change. It's unsurprising that the majority of us are averse to our uniform and believe that it should be abolished. We feel that a uniform prevents individual expression and represents an unnecessary level of control. It can also be extremely expensive. However, a small handful of pupils did seem to praise the restrictive nature of a school uniform — one student seemed to believe that having a uniform makes all students equal and may even foster a sense of pride in the school.

You think you have it tough...

a) Some sentences in the text are written in the first person plural. How do they affect the reader?

....

....

b) i) Describe the tone of the text using two adjectives.

....

ii) How does the tone influence how the reader feels? Explain your answer.

....

....

....

c) What is your opinion of school uniform after reading the text? Explain your answer.

....

....

....

d) Do you think the author provides a balanced view of the topic? Explain your answer.

NOW TRY THIS — How many other pros and cons can you think of for school uniform? Jot them all down, then have a go at writing a short text to explain your point of view. You should try to be as balanced as possible in your arguments and make sure you include an introduction and a conclusion.

Section 2: Reading — Non-Fiction Texts

The Author's Intentions

How a text is written often gives away clues about the author's intentions. If you look closely at the language they use and the overall tone of the text, you should be able to work out what they're trying to do.

1. Extracts A-D are from a blog by a travel writer.

   A From the outside, the cathedral looks rather drab — its stone gargoyles are caked in dirt, and you can barely see the intricate carving of the stonework. Inside, however, it's like a completely different building. The stained-glass windows are wonderfully detailed, not to mention rich in vibrant colours.

   B Situated just a short walk from the station, the memorial garden overlooks one of the busiest stretches of the river. It's not the quietest of places, nor is it the prettiest. Boats are constantly to-ing and fro-ing, many of the shrubs are overgrown, and the paths are littered with dead leaves and twigs. Even the birds choose not to linger for too long.

   C The castle is largely intact, with small portions which have fallen into ruin. There's a fascinating exhibit about the castle's history, which is well worth seeing. I could have spent all day looking at the artefacts! The ramparts offer a spectacular view of the landscape, particularly of the smooth, rolling hills in the north.

   D The colossal statues are a rather intimidating presence in the central square. It's quite an unpleasant feeling to stand right beneath them — you can almost feel them looking down on you. But from a distance, you can begin to appreciate how magnificent they are. They appear to be watching over the city, guarding it from unwanted intruders.

   a) i) Which tourist attraction does the author present as...

   ...interesting? ⟶ ....

   ...disappointing? ⟶ ....

   ...unsettling? ⟶ ....

   ...surprising? ⟶ ....

   ii) Using details from the extracts, explain why you chose your answers to part i).

   b) i) Which tourist attraction does the author present most positively?

   ....

   ii) How do they do this? Explain your answer using examples from the relevant extract.

Section 3: Reading — Fiction and Plays

The next section is basically a load of stories and plays for you to read, with one tiny catch — you also need to answer some questions on them. This section will hone your ability to identify and analyse the effect of the different features of fiction texts. These warm-up questions should start you off nicely...

Before you Start

1. The extract below is from the story *Run For Your Life*.

   > A chorus of excited chatter echoed around the start line as the runners began to line up. Anna could feel the adrenaline rushing through her veins. Her legs were like coiled springs, ready to launch her forward on the 'b' of the bang. She took a few deep breaths and focused on the road ahead, trying to block out the other competitors' nervous shoves and shuffles. The figures in the crowd blurred together and everything in Anna's sight became obscured, except the road ahead. All she had to do now was stay focused.
   >
   > "Anna!" The shout shattered Anna's concentration, sending ice-cold dread washing through her. She'd know that voice anywhere. Anna frantically scanned the crowd, heart pounding in her chest, until she found him. Agent One was staring straight at her.
   >
   > Anna trembled as she looked into his vacant eyes. "How did he...?" Then the gun fired. The pack of runners lurched forward. Anna shot ahead instinctively — a bolt for freedom. He'd finally found her. She couldn't — wouldn't — allow herself to be caught. Not this time. Not like this.

   a) Write one sentence that summarises how Anna feels at the beginning of the extract.

   ....

   ....

   b) What does the author mean by "on the 'b' of the bang"?

   ....

   c) Why do you think the author uses short sentences at the end of the extract?

   ....

   ....

   d) i) Tick the box next to the phrase that best describes Anna at the end of the extract.

   confident and driven ☐   confused and hopeless ☐   afraid but determined ☐

   ii) Explain your answer to part d).

   e) Explain how the mood of the extract changes after Anna sees Agent One.

Finding Evidence in the Text

People say there's no right answer in English literature, but a <u>good</u> answer is one that is based on evidence found in the text. This might be a quote, detail or example, or something you've inferred from the wider text.

1. The extract below is adapted from *Emma* by Jane Austen. Emma is a wealthy young woman who has a romantic interest in Frank Churchill, the son of a local landowner. She has just found out that Frank is engaged to someone else.

   > "You have some news to hear that will rather surprise you," said Emma.
   >
   > Mr Knightley replied, "If you mean Frank Churchill's proposal to Miss Fairfax, I know already."
   >
   > "How is it possible?" cried Emma, turning her glowing cheeks towards him.
   >
   > "I was given a brief account of what had happened this morning."
   >
   > Emma was quite relieved, and could presently say, with a little more composure, "*You* probably have been less surprised than any of us, for you have had your suspicions. — I have not forgotten that you once tried to give me a caution about Frank Churchill. — I wish I had attended to it — but — (with a sinking voice and a heavy sigh) I seem to have been doomed to blindness."
   >
   > For a moment or two nothing was said, and she was unsuspicious of having excited any particular interest, till she found her arm drawn within his, and pressed against his heart, and heard him thus saying, in a tone of great sensibility, speaking low, "Time, my dearest Emma, time will heal the wound. — Your own excellent sense — your exertions for your father's sake — I know you will not allow yourself —." Her arm was pressed again, as he added, in a more broken and subdued accent, "The feelings of the warmest friendship — Indignation — Abominable scoundrel!" — And in a louder, steadier tone, he concluded with, "He will soon be gone. They will soon be in Yorkshire. I am sorry for *her*. She deserves a better fate."

   a) i) What news does Emma want to tell Mr Knightley?

   ....

   ii) Why isn't Mr Knightley as surprised by the news as Emma expects? Circle one option.

   | He was suspicious of Frank Churchill. | He had already heard it from someone else. | Frank Churchill may have told him as they are close friends. |

   b) Write down the part of the text that shows:

How Emma feels about ignoring Mr Knightley's warning	
Mr Knightley's view of Frank Churchill	
Mr Knightley's view of Miss Fairfax	

   c) How can you tell that Mr Knightley cares deeply about Emma?
   Use details from the text to support your answer.

Summarising

Summarising is briefly rewriting the important points of a paragraph, or a whole story, in your own words. Make sure that you carefully select only the key bits before you dive into writing your summary.

1. The extract below is from the story *Fractures*.

   > Gemma slumped into the bus seat, clutching her rucksack. The empty seat beside her felt like a neon sign, garishly taunting her in capital letters: 'FRIENDLESS'. Self-consciously, she shifted her rucksack from her lap onto the forlorn chair. At least now she could seem deliberately, defiantly, anti-social rather than utterly abandoned.
   >
   > Abandoned was the right word, Gemma thought to herself. Deserted, forsaken, rejected, ditched, dumped... the adjectives piled up melodramatically in her mind. For years they had sat together, chatted together, laughed together; people had joked that she and Jodie were practically joined at the hip. They had even pretended to be twins on more than one occasion. But now Gemma felt like a half-thing, useless and alone.
   >
   > Really, she should have seen the separation coming. Their friendship had always been just like a bad Hollywood film — 'two girls, the sports freak and the maths geek, become unlikely friends' — and, like in those films, was doomed to failure from the opening scene. The fractures had opened gradually, then all at once, as their differences had got the better of them. Jodie had missed the bus home more and more, staying late for hockey practice or taking a lift home with her team mates. Now she'd begun avoiding Gemma on the bus to school as well.
   >
   > This morning was no different. Gemma glanced up as Jodie walked past her seat — the seat they had shared for years. Jodie's eyes flickered over her as if she were a ghost.

   a) In your own words, summarise Gemma's feelings in the paragraph starting "Abandoned".

   ....

   ....

   b) Write one sentence summarising Gemma's relationship with Jodie when they were younger.

   ....

   ....

   c) Summarise why Gemma and Jodie have grown apart.

   d) i) Tick the sentence below that best summarises the whole text.

      Gemma and Jodie were best friends but they fell out suddenly. ☐

      Gemma feels upset because she has grown apart from her best friend. ☐

      Gemma saves a seat for Jodie on the bus, but her friend ignores her. ☐

      ii) Explain why you chose your answer to part i).

Working Out What's Going On

Being able to infer — aka find hidden details in a piece of writing — is an essential skill when you're reading texts. You need to work out what's implied by the text, as well as understanding its surface meaning.

1. The extract below is from *We See Everything* by William Sutcliffe.

> It's a long time since I saw this much sky. Only in the largest bomb sites or out here can you see anything that resembles a horizon, or feel the sky to be more than narrow corridors of air hanging over each street.
>
> The clouds are high today, distant pale streaks against which the drones are easier to see than ever, giant locusts with digital bug eyes which circle over London day and night, watching everything we do.
>
> The closest one banks directly above me, changing pitch slightly as it turns back towards the city.
>
> Sunshine prickles deliciously against the skin of my face. Beads of sweat begin to form on my forehead and upper lip, and I fight the instinct to wipe them away, thinking of how they will evaporate, then float away out of this prison-city: a tiny part of me staging an invisible escape.
>
> On the underside of a leaf, I notice a ladybird. I haven't seen one for years. Reaching out an index finger, I coax the insect on to the back of my hand. It ambles towards my wrist, its feet giving such a light tickle that I can't be sure I've actually felt anything at all.

a) Tick a box to show whether each sentence is true or false.

   True   False

   i) Conflict has shaped the landscape.

   ii) The narrator is under constant surveillance.

   iii) The narrator doesn't know where they are.

b) Write out the part of the text that shows you the narrator is enjoying the weather.

   ....

c) The narrator hasn't seen a ladybird "for years". Explain what this suggests about London.

   ....

   ....

d) How does the author suggest that the narrator feels trapped?
   Explain your answer using evidence from the text.

NOW TRY THIS — Now that you've worked out what's happening in the text above, write a few paragraphs about what you think happened before this point in the story. What did the landscape used to look like? What would the narrator have been doing? Use your answers on this page to help you.

© Not to be photocopied   Section 3: Reading — Fiction and Plays

Structure

The structure of a story isn't just its beginning, middle and end. Structure describes anything from the overall order of the events in the text right down to its syntax (how words are arranged in a sentence).

1. The extract below is from *The World According to Talia*.

> An explanation:
>
> ~~It's probably my fault.~~ It isn't my fault.
>
> In my defence, Mr and Mrs Green didn't tell me what time they'd get back from the theatre. ~~They might have mentioned 8pm, but how was I meant to remember?~~
>
> Okay, so I know that the children should have been in bed by seven. I know Mrs Green warned me that giving them sweets would make them hyper. I know that playing hide-and-seek was probably a bad idea. But I *didn't* know that ~~the idiot~~ Sam, after devouring a bag of lemon sherbets, would attempt to climb out of the window.
>
> Apparently, to a seven-year-old boy, a windowsill is the perfect hiding place.
>
> So that's how I've ended up here: Sam clinging to a ledge outside a first-floor window; his parents standing horrified and screaming in the garden; me on the landing ~~frozen in a state of complete panic~~ calmly considering what I should do.
>
> Not exactly the ideal start to my baby-sitting career.
>
> The story so far:
>
> Let's rewind. Yes, I may be in a *slightly* sticky situation right now, but that doesn't mean I can forget my manners. I'm Talia — pleased to meet you.

a) Which of the following describes the structure of the extract? Circle one option.

| The narrative follows chronological order. | There is a flashback in the narrative. | The extract ends with a flashforward. |

b) What do you think is the effect of the author using headings?

....

c) "I know" is repeated several times in the text. What is the effect of this repetition?

....

....

d) Why do you think some of the text has been crossed out?

....

....

e) Talia doesn't introduce herself until the end of the extract. What effect does this have?

f) Explain whether you think the extract is an effective opening to a story. Use your answers to the questions above to help you.

Section 3: Reading — Fiction and Plays

Themes

The theme of my birthday party was 'Under the Sea' — we had a <u>whale</u> of a time. Ahem. Themes are the big ideas behind a text — you need to be able to explain how different bits of the text relate to its theme.

1. The extract below is adapted from *Oliver Twist* by Charles Dickens. One of the main themes in *Oliver Twist* is crime and morality.

   > The Dodger made a sudden stop; and, laying his finger on his lip, drew his companions back again, with the greatest caution and circumspection.
   >
   > "Do you see that old cove at the book-stall?" the Dodger said.
   >
   > "The old gentleman over the way?" said Oliver. "Yes, I see him."
   >
   > "He'll do," said the Dodger.
   >
   > "A prime plant," observed Master Charley Bates.
   >
   > Oliver looked from one to the other, with the greatest surprise; but he was not permitted to make any inquiries; for the two boys walked stealthily across the road, and slunk close behind the old gentleman towards whom his attention had been directed.
   >
   > What was Oliver's horror and alarm as he stood a few paces off, looking on with his eyelids as wide open as they would possibly go, to see the Dodger plunge his hand into the old gentleman's pocket, and draw from thence a handkerchief! To see him hand the same to Charley Bates; and finally to behold them, both running away round the corner at full speed!
   >
   > He stood, for a moment, with the blood so tingling through all his veins from terror, that he felt as if he were in a burning fire; then, confused and frightened, he took to his heels; and, not knowing what he did, made off as fast as he could lay his feet to the ground.

   a) How do the events of the extract relate to the theme of crime and morality?

   ....

   ....

   b) Tick a box to show whether each sentence is true or false.

	True	False
i) The Dodger and Charley Bates use criminal slang.	☐	☐
ii) Oliver was already aware that his friends were criminals.	☐	☐
iii) The Dodger and Charley Bates use Oliver as a diversion.	☐	☐

   c) How does the author suggest that the Dodger and Charley Bates are experienced thieves?

   ....

   ....

   ....

   d) i) How does Oliver feel about crime? Explain your answer using details from the text.

   ii) Explain how Oliver's attitude is different to the other boys in the extract.

Language Techniques

Alliteration, metaphors, similes, personification, onomatopoeia... writers have an enormous inventory of different language techniques up their sleeves which they can use to make the reader feel a certain way.

1. The extract below is from *How to Make a Bird* by Martine Murray.
   The narrator has run away from home because she feels like she doesn't fit in.

   > The moon was lying pale and quivery in the sky, like a bony fingermark on a black cloth. The houses were hushed and still and I was telling myself there was no reason to feel sad, not even for the wings, or the way the moon was fading, getting thin like tissue. There wasn't even one piece of brightness to ache over. The fields were like crinkled-up grey blankets huddled over a sleeping earth. Harry Jacob's house looked grim, all bitten by the blackness. During the day it was the colour of a mint chew, and perched awkwardly on its bald grass slope as if it hadn't quite settled. Now it had sunk smugly into the night's shadows and it peered down at me as if it knew what I was doing, standing there alone in the darkness. In the midst of the bleating crickets and cracking thin limbs of the trees, I could almost hear the house letting out a muffled sneery snort, like my mother used to when I said what I thought of one thing or another. Well, don't pretend, I felt like saying to Harry Jacob's green house, don't pretend that you belong now. Just because the night has made you the same colour as all the other houses, don't pretend to be serious, because as soon as the light comes up you'll still be an old green house that doesn't look right.

   a) i) Draw lines to show which technique each phrase is an example of.

Phrase	Technique
The fields were like crinkled-up grey blankets	personification
the bleating crickets and cracking thin limbs of the trees	simile
the house letting out a muffled sneery snort	onomatopoeia

   ii) What is the effect of each of the techniques in part i)?

   b) The author uses two similes to describe the moon.
   Underline the similes, then explain why you think the author chose them.

   ....

   ....

   ....

   c) How does the author make Harry Jacob's house seem alive? Explain your answer.

   ....

   ....

   d) Explain how the description of the house reflects the narrator's feelings in the extract.

   NOW TRY THIS Using the extract above as inspiration, write a paragraph describing a building that you are familiar with. Make sure you include as many of the language techniques covered on this page as possible. Try to think about how the building makes you feel as well as how it looks.

Understanding the Characters

They say it's what's on the inside that counts, and that's true for characters too. It's not enough just to know what characters look like — you need to consider how they think and act, and what this tells you about them.

1. The extract below is from *A Skinful of Shadows* by Frances Hardinge.

    > Mother was always strangest when something was important. It was as though she kept this other self, this wilful, incomprehensible, otherworldly self, in the clothes chest below her Sunday best, for use in emergencies. At these times she was not Mother, she was Margaret. Her eyes seemed deeper, her hair beneath her cap thicker and witchier, her attention on something that Makepeace could not see.

    Tick a box to show whether each sentence is true or false.   True   False

    a) There are different sides to Mother's personality. ☐ ☐

    b) The narrator doesn't fully understand Mother. ☐ ☐

    c) Mother changes randomly and unpredictably. ☐ ☐

2. The extract below is from *Red Leaves* by Sita Brahmachari.

    > 'Keep distant from the wood. Make sure you stay close by the road,' were the last words that Shalini spoke to him as he walked out of the door.
    >
    > Or what? Zak asked himself as he entered the rusted metal gates that bordered the woodland. He'd always been happiest in the woods that backed on to his old house, with his dad, hunting for the best place to build a den or pitching stumps for a game of cricket. It hadn't been that long ago since they'd walked hand in hand singing childish songs.
    >
    > A small red leaf wafted down between the branches. If I catch that leaf it'll make everything go back to normal. He rarely missed a catch. He held out his hand, but just as it was about to land safely in his palm, the leaf caught on the wind and floated away.
    >
    > Zak sighed. What's the matter with me? How can catching a falling leaf change anything one way or the other? Except that was just how he felt these days — like a leaf being wafted on winds that other people had whipped up, with no way of knowing where he would land.

    a) i) Why does Zak make a wish on the falling leaf?

    ....

    ii) What does this action suggest about Zak?

    b) Briefly describe Zak's relationship with his dad, giving an example to back up your point.

    c) How does the author show that Zak doesn't feel in control of his life?
    Explain your answer using details from the text.

© Not to be photocopied   Section 3: Reading — Fiction and Plays

Understanding the Characters

3. The extract below is from a stage adaptation of *Kes* by Barry Hines and Lawrence Till.

> *A customer has a book stamped out. Billy just stands looking round in the library.*

Billy   Can I get a book now then?

Librarian   You'll have to take one of these forms home first for your father to sign.

Billy   My dad's away.

Librarian   You'll have to wait till he comes home then.

Billy   I don't mean away like that. I mean he's left home.

Librarian   Oh I see . . . well in that case your mother'll have to sign it.

Billy   She's at work.

Librarian   She can sign it when she comes home, can't she?

Billy   She'll not be home till tea time and it's Sunday tomorrow. I want a book today.

Librarian   Then you'll just have to wait, won't you?

Billy   Just let me go an' see 'f you've got one, an' if you have I'll sit down at one o' them tables and read it.

Librarian   You can't. You're not a member.

Billy   Nobody'll know.

Librarian   It's against the rules.

Billy   Go on. I'll bring you this paper back on Monday then.

> *Another customer hands a book to the librarian to be stamped out. They chat pleasantly about the weather. Billy sees the zoology shelf and goes to it. He quickly finds a book about hawks, puts it under his jacket and quickly goes out of the library, past the two still talking at the desk.*

Billy   Ta-ra.

(Speech bubble: "This would make more sense if I could read...")

a) i) Tick the two adjectives that best describe Billy in this extract.

    impatient ☐   disappointed ☐   impolite ☐   daring ☐

   ii) Using details from the extract, explain why you chose your answers for part i).

b) Billy steals the book then says "Ta-ra". Explain what this suggests about him.

....

....

c) What impression do you get of the librarian from this extract? Explain your answer.

Now Try This: Now it's your go — write a paragraph describing a character. Make sure you don't just describe what your character looks like — you also need to write about what they do, say and think. Consider what their actions and how they speak to others might suggest about their character.

Section 3: Reading — Fiction and Plays

Understanding the Setting

The setting is where a story takes place, but it's also much more than that. The setting affects everything from the story's atmosphere to how the characters act — so don't forget to comment on it in your answers.

1. The extract below is from *Island Songs* by Alex Wheatle.

   > The cooling breeze that drifted in from the Caribbean sea was still and Joseph guessed that the seasonal wind and rains would surely come soon; he sensed it in the balmy aroma of the soil. He looked up again and wondered if the terrain he was studying locked away as many secrets as he did, nightmarish memories that he had yet to even tell his wife. He turned slowly to view the ramshackle dwellings of villagers who had constructed their homes precariously on steep hillsides and astride grassy escarpments, the patchwork of corrugated zinc roofs reflecting the light. A hot Jamaican sun was setting, but on this secluded part of the north of the island, two thousand feet above sea level, the yellow eye didn't rage as it did on the flat southern plains, where most of the sugar plantations were located and where the crocodiles swam silently in swampy rivers thick with reeds.

   a) Where is this extract set? Circle the correct option.

   | the Caribbean sea | Jamaica | a sugar plantation | the southern plains |

   b) Write down the part of the text that shows you that the extract takes place in the evening.

   ....

   c) Write down two examples of sensory language from the extract that describe the setting.

   ....

   ....

   d) What impression of the villagers' dwellings do you get from this extract?
   Use examples from the text to support your answer.

   ....

   ....

   e) Compare how the two sides of the island are described in the extract.

   ....

   ....

   f) How does the author make the southern side of the island sound threatening?
   Explain your answer using details from the extract.

Understanding the Setting

2. The extract below is from *The Portrait of a Lady* by Henry James.

> The front of the house, overlooking that portion of the lawn with which we are concerned, was not the entrance-front; this was in quite another quarter. Privacy here reigned supreme, and the wide carpet of turf that covered the level hill-top seemed but the extension of a luxurious interior. The great still oaks and beeches flung down a shade as dense as that of velvet curtains; and the place was furnished, like a room, with cushioned seats, with rich-coloured rugs, with the books and papers that lay upon the grass. The river was at some distance; where the ground began to slope, the lawn, properly speaking, ceased. But it was none the less a charming walk down to the water.

a) What is the lawn outside the house compared to?

....

b) Write down some imagery from the extract that suggests the garden is a private place.

....

c) i) Tick the box next to the adjective that best summarises the setting of the extract above.

quiet ☐   neglected ☐   cosy ☐   intimidating ☐   grand ☐

ii) Explain your answer to part i), using details from the text.

....

....

....

d) What does the setting suggest about the people who live there? Explain your answer.

....

....

e) Write down an adjective that describes the atmosphere of the setting. Explain why you chose this adjective, using details from the extract.

NOW TRY THIS — Imagine you're writing a fairytale. Write a paragraph describing the setting of the story in as much detail as possible. Make sure you think about how your choice of setting could affect the text. Then, write a short explanation about why your setting would be suitable for a fairytale.

Interpreting Plays

In drama (unlike most stories), the playwright doesn't usually tell the audience exactly what's happening. Instead, you need to use the dialogue and stage directions as clues to work out what's going on. Sneaky.

1. The extract below is from *Our Day Out* by Willy Russell.

> DRIVER: Right. Just stop there. Don't move.
> KID: Miss said we could get on.
> DRIVER: Oh, did she now?
> KIDS: Yeh.
> DRIVER: Well, let me tell youse lot something now. Miss isn't the driver of this coach. I am. An' if I say y' don't get on, y' don't get on.
> MRS KAY: Is anything wrong, Driver?
> DRIVER: Are these children in your charge, madam?
> MRS KAY: Yes.
> DRIVER: Well y' haven't checked them, have y'?
> MRS KAY: Checked them? Checked them for what?
> DRIVER: Chocolate an' lemonade! We don't allow it. I've seen it on other coaches madam; fifty-two vomitin' kids… it's no joke. No, I'm sorry, we don't allow that.
> MRS KAY: (*to SUSAN*) Here comes Mr Happiness. All right, Driver… I'll check for you.
> (*to KIDS*) …Now listen, everyone. If anybody's got any chocolate or lemonade I want you to put your hands up.
> (*A sea of dumb faces and unraised hands. MRS KAY smiles at the DRIVER*)
> There you are, Driver. All right?
> DRIVER: No, it's not all right. Y' can't just take their word for it. They have to be searched. Y' can't just believe kids.
> *Pause. MRS KAY stares at him. She could blow up but she doesn't.*

a) Tick all the adjectives that could be used to describe the bus driver.

restrained ☐   irritable ☐   well-mannered ☐   inflexible ☐   amiable ☐

b) Explain your answer to part a), using details from the text.

....

....

c) Why do you think Mrs Kay calls the driver "Mr Happiness"?

....

....

d) What does the stage direction "*She could blow up but she doesn't*" suggest about Mrs Kay's character? Explain your answer.

Interpreting Plays

2. The extract below is adapted from *The Tempest* by William Shakespeare.

> MIRANDA: Do you love me?
>
> FERDINAND: O heaven, O earth, bear witness to this sound,
> And crown what I profess with kind event*,
> If I speak true! If hollowly, invert
> What best is boded me to mischief!* I,
> Beyond all limit of what else i' th' world,
> Do love, prize, honour you.
>
> MIRANDA: I am a fool
> To weep at what I am glad of.
>
> PROSPERO: (aside) Fair encounter
> Of two most rare affections! Heavens rain grace
> On that which breeds between 'em!
>
> FERDINAND: Wherefore* weep you?
>
> MIRANDA: At mine unworthiness. Hence*, bashful cunning,
> And prompt me, plain and holy innocence!
> I am your wife, if you will marry me,
> If not, I'll die your maid.
>
> FERDINAND: My mistress, dearest,
> And I thus humble ever.
>
> MIRANDA: My husband, then?
>
> FERDINAND: Ay, with a heart as willing
> As bondage e'er of freedom.

In The Tempest, *Miranda and Ferdinand fall in love at first sight. In this scene, they declare their love for one another while Miranda's father, Prospero, watches in secret.*

*crown what I profess with kind event — reward me

*invert / What best is boded me to mischief — turn everything good that could happen to me to bad

*Wherefore — why

*Hence — go away

So basically I really really love you!

Yup, you already said that...

a) Write out the part of the extract that backs up each point below.

   i) Miranda cries because she is happy.

   ....

   ii) Ferdinand is very eager to marry Miranda.

   ....

b) Does Prospero approve of Miranda and Ferdinand's relationship? Explain your answer.

   ....

   ....

c) How does Ferdinand's language emphasise his love for Miranda?
   Use quotes from the text to back up your points

NOW TRY THIS — The best way to test whether you really understand Shakespearean language is to rewrite it in your own words. Rewrite the extract above in simple, modern English. If there's a bit you don't understand, have a guess at what it might mean — use the bits you *do* understand to work it out.

Staging and Performance

Staging is all about how a play is presented on stage. Performance is (you guessed it) how actors perform the play. There are two important parts to performance: how the characters <u>speak</u> and how they <u>move</u>.

1. The extract below is adapted from *Macbeth* by William Shakespeare. Macbeth has recently had his friend, Banquo, killed, and he starts to hallucinate as a result of his guilt.

   > *Enter the GHOST OF BANQUO and sits in Macbeth's place*
   > ROSSE: Please't your highness
   > To grace us with your royal company?
   > MACBETH: The table's full.
   > LENNOX: Here is a place reserved, sir.
   > MACBETH: Which of you have done this?
   > LORDS: What, my good lord?
   > MACBETH: Thou canst not say I did it; never shake
   > Thy gory locks at me!
   > ROSSE: Gentlemen, rise, his highness is not well.
   > *LADY MACBETH joins the Lords.*
   > LADY MACBETH: Sit, worthy friends. My lord is often thus*,
   > And hath* been from his youth. Pray you, keep seat.
   > Feed, and regard him not. (*To Macbeth*) Are you a man?
   > MACBETH: Ay, and a bold one, that dare look on that
   > Which might appal the devil.
   > LADY MACBETH: O proper stuff!
   > This is the very painting of your fear;
   > Why do you make such faces? When all's done,
   > You look but on a stool.
   > MACBETH: Prithee*, see there! Behold, look, lo*! How say you?
   > (*To Ghost*) Why, what care I? If thou canst nod, speak too.

   The way a play is performed affects the audience's response to it. Think about how this extract could be performed in different ways to create different effects.

   *thus — like this
   *hath — has
   *Prithee — Please
   *lo — look

   a) Underline the parts of the extract where the Lords are told how to move or act.

   b) i) How do you think Macbeth feels in the lines beginning "Thou canst not"?

      ....

      ii) How do you think the actor should speak and move to emphasise Macbeth's feelings?

      ....

      ....

   c) Write down how the actor playing Lady Macbeth could speak and move to emphasise her feelings in the lines beginning "O proper stuff!" Explain your answer.

   d) A director could choose to show Banquo's ghost on stage, so that the audience can see it too, or not show it on stage, so that only Macbeth can see it. Do you think the ghost of Banquo should be shown on stage? Explain your answer.

What You Think

This time, it's all about you — how does the text make you feel? How does the author achieve this effect? E.g. CGP books make me feel happy and informed because they contain great jokes and loads of facts.

1. The extract below is from *The Book Thief* by Markus Zusak.

> **HERE IS A SMALL FACT**
>
> **You are going to die.**
>
> I am in all truthfulness attempting to be cheerful about this whole topic, though most people find themselves hindered in believing me, no matter my protestations. Please, trust me. I most definitely *can* be cheerful. I can be amiable. Agreeable. Affable. And that's only the As. Just don't ask me to be nice. Nice has nothing to do with me.
>
> **REACTION TO THE AFOREMENTIONED FACT**
>
> **Does this worry you?**
>
> **I urge you — don't be afraid.**
>
> **I'm nothing if not fair.**
>
> Of course, an introduction.
>   A beginning.
>   Where are my manners?
>   I could introduce myself properly, but it's not really necessary. You will know me well enough and soon enough, depending on a diverse range of variables. It suffices to say that at some point in time, I will be standing over you, as genially as possible. Your soul will be in my arms.

a) Who do you think the narrator is in this extract?

....

b) i) What is the tone of the extract? Circle the correct option.

| negative and unfriendly | cold but reassuring | serious but optimistic |

ii) Using details from the text, explain your answer to part i).

....

....

....

c) The extract is written in the first person. What effect does this have on the reader?

....

....

d) What impression do you get of the narrator? How do they make you feel? Use details from the extract to explain your answer.

Section 3: Reading — Fiction and Plays

Section 4: Reading — Poetry

Some poets write straightforward poems with obvious meanings. However, other poets may expect you to interpret your own meanings from more subtle clues. Don't let that put you off though — as long as you can offer evidence and an explanation to support your point, you'll be absolutely fine. I believe in you.

Before you Start

1. The poem below is *Remember* by Christina Rossetti.

   > Remember me when I am gone away,
   >   Gone far away into the silent land;
   >   When you can no more hold me by the hand,
   > Nor I half turn to go yet turning stay.
   > Remember me when no more day by day
   >   You tell me of our future that you plann'd:
   >   Only remember me; you understand
   > It will be late to counsel* then or pray.
   > Yet if you should forget me for a while
   >   And afterwards remember, do not grieve:
   >   For if the darkness and corruption leave
   > A vestige* of the thoughts that once I had,
   > Better by far you should forget and smile
   >   Than that you should remember and be sad.

   Speech bubble: Remember me when I need a wash, Need a wash because I smell...

   *counsel — advise
   *vestige — a trace of something that no longer exists

   a) What do you think "the silent land" is?

   ....

   b) Who do you think the narrator is addressing in the poem?

   ....

   c) Which of the following techniques is used in this poem? Tick one option.

   alliteration ☐   repetition ☐   simile ☐

   d) Give one example of the technique you ticked in part c), then explain its effect.

   ....
   ....
   ....

   e) What do you think is the narrator's main message in the poem? Explain your answer.

Working Out What's Going On

You might have to think a bit more carefully when reading a poem to work out what's really going on. Read through a poem at least a couple of times before answering any questions to make sure you understand it.

1. The poem below is *Water Picture* by May Swenson.

   > In the pond in the park
   > all things are doubled:
   > Long buildings hang and
   > wriggle gently. Chimneys
   > are bent legs bouncing
   > on clouds below. A flag
   > wags like a fishhook
   > down there in the sky.
   >
   > The arched stone bridge
   > is an eye, with underlid
   > in the water. In its lens
   > dip crinkled heads with hats
   > that don't fall off. Dogs go by,
   > barking on their backs.
   > A baby, taken to feed the
   > ducks, dangles upside-down,
   > a pink balloon for a buoy.
   >
   > Treetops deploy a haze of
   > cherry bloom for roots,
   > where birds coast belly-up
   > in the glass bowl of a hill;
   > from its bottom a bunch
   > of peanut-munching children
   > is suspended by their
   > sneakers, waveringly.
   >
   > A swan, with twin necks
   > forming the figure 3,
   > steers between two dimpled
   > towers doubled. Fondly
   > hissing, she kisses herself,
   > and all the scene is troubled:
   > water-windows splinter,
   > tree-limbs tangle, the bridge
   > folds like a fan.

   a) Tick the box that provides the best summary of the poem.

The poet is describing the park's reflection in the pond.	The poet is describing what the park looks like underwater.	The poet is describing what the pond looks like from the sky.
☐	☐	☐

   b) i) Write down a quote from the poem that supports your answer to part a).

   ....

   ii) Explain how the quote you have chosen supports your answer to part a).

   ....

   ....

   c) What happens to make the scene "troubled" in the fourth stanza?

   ....

   ....

   d) In your own words, summarise what is happening in the second stanza.

Structure

If you're asked about the structure of a poem, you need to look at its stanzas and the length of its lines as well as its rhythm and rhyming pattern. These features often contribute to the meaning of a poem.

1. The poem below is *Russian Doll* by Rachel Rooney.

   > All you see is outside me: my painted smile,
   > the rosy-posy shell, the fluttery eyes.
   > A butter-won't-melt-in-my-mouth-type me.
   >
   > But inside there's another me, bored till playtime.
   > The wasting paper, daytime dreamer.
   > A can't-be-bothered-sort-of-me.
   >
   > And inside there's another me, full of cheek.
   > The quick, slick joker with a poking tongue.
   > A class-clown-funny-one-of me.
   >
   > And inside there's another me who's smaller, scared.
   > The scurrying, worrying, yes miss whisperer.
   > A wouldn't-say-boo-to-a-goosey me.
   >
   > And inside there's another me, all cross and bothered.
   > The scowling hot-head, stamping feet.
   > A didn't-do-it-blameless me.
   >
   > And inside there's another me, forever jealous,
   > who never gets enough, compared.
   > A grass-is-always-greener me.
   >
   > And deepest down, kept secretly,
   > a tiny, solid skittle doll.
   > The girl that hides inside of me.

   A Russian doll is a set of hollow dolls of different sizes that fit inside each other.

   a) Why do you think the poem begins with "outside me" and ends with the girl "inside of me"?

   ....
   ....
   ....

   b) How is the structure of the stanzas in the poem like a Russian doll?

   ....
   ....
   ....

   c) i) Circle the internal rhymes in the lines below.

   > The quick, slick joker with a poking tongue.

   > The scurrying, worrying, yes miss whisperer.

   Internal rhyme is when words or parts of words within a line rhyme.

   ii) What is the effect of using internal rhyme in the poem?

   d) i) How is the final stanza's structure different to the rest of the poem?

   ii) Explain why you think the poet has done this.

Themes

So, a theme is an idea or concept that appears in a piece of writing (like love, nature, death or war). Surely that means a theme park is a place where poetry fans can discuss the themes of their favourite poems?

1. Poem A is *Everyone Sang* by Siegfried Sassoon.
Poem B is *They dropped like Flakes* by Emily Dickinson.

Sassoon's poem was written a year after World War One ended. Dickinson's poem is about the American Civil War (1861-1865).

A Everyone suddenly burst out singing;
And I was filled with such delight
As prisoned birds must find in freedom,
Winging wildly across the white
Orchards and dark-green fields; on - on - and
    out of sight.

Everyone's voice was suddenly lifted;
And beauty came like the setting sun:
My heart was shaken with tears; and horror
Drifted away ... O, but Everyone
Was a bird; and the song was wordless; the
    singing will never be done.

B They dropped like Flakes —
They dropped like Stars —
Like Petals from a Rose —
When suddenly across the June
A wind with fingers — goes —

They perished in the Seamless Grass —
No eye could find the place —
But God can summon every face
On his Repealless*-List.

*repealless — endless or eternal

a) i) Tick the main emotion that is expressed in *Everyone Sang*.

sadness ☐   anger ☐   happiness ☐   excitement ☐

ii) How does the narrator use figurative language to express this emotion?

....

....

iii) Why do you think the narrator feels this way?

....

....

b) Re-read the last stanza of *They dropped like Flakes*. What do you think the poet is suggesting about those who die fighting in a war?

....

....

c) In *They dropped like Flakes*, nature is used to refer to soldiers dying during the war. Why do you think the poet does this?

NOW TRY THIS — Just because two poems share a theme, it doesn't always mean that they have the same purpose or present the theme in a similar way. Write a short paragraph that compares the attitude that each poem's narrator has towards war. Use evidence from both poems to support your answer.

Section 4: Reading — Poetry © Not to be photocopied

Voice

No, I'm not talking about that performance voice we use when we read aloud. In poetry, voice refers to the poem's speaker and how they speak. So, in a poem about poetry, the voice could be a joyful Year 8 pupil.

1. The poem below is *Right To Be* by Amyra León.

I got the right to be	May we raise our voices till
Got the right to be	Peace dawns on us
Got the right to be me	Till the worlds slaves
Unapologetically	Are set free
	and equality is no longer a dream
Limbs swaying in the wind	
To the sound of crimson	Till we can scream
Drowning the sea	At the top of our lungs
Setting my people free	And truly believe
Children of the sun	That we got the right to be
Of the deep atlantic ocean	Got the right to be
Our ancestors died	Got the right to be free
So we could breathe	Unapologetically
In the air of freedom	

    Amyra León is a Black American musician and poet who explores themes such as social and racial inequality.

    a) Who do you think the speaker is in this poem? Who are they addressing?

    ....

    ....

    b) i) Is the voice of the poem formal or informal? Find a quote to support your answer.

    ....

    ii) What effect does this have on the reader?

    ....

    ....

    ....

    c) The perspective of the poem shifts from first person singular at the start to first person plural by the end. What effect does this have?

    d) i) Write down three adjectives that you would use to describe the tone of the poem.

    ....

    ii) Explain why you have chosen these adjectives. Use quotes to support your answer.

© Not to be photocopied

Section 4: Reading — Poetry

Techniques

Poets use techniques (like similes, metaphors and personification) to express key messages. They can help the poet relay something complex by describing it in a way that's easier for the reader to imagine.

1. The poem below is *Taal* by Imtiaz Dharker.

A taal is a traditional rhythmic pattern in classical Indian music.

> This music will not sit in straight lines.
> The notes refuse to perch on wires
>
> but move in rhythm with the dancer
> round the face of the clock,
> through the dandelion head of time.
>
> We feel blown free, but circle back
> to be in love, to touch and part
> and meet again, spun
>
> past the face of the moon, the precise
> underpinning of stars. The cycle begins
> with one and ends with one,
>
> dha dhin dhin dha. There must be
> other feet in step with us, an underbeat,
> a voice that keeps count, not yours or mine.
>
> This music is playing us.
> We are playing with time.

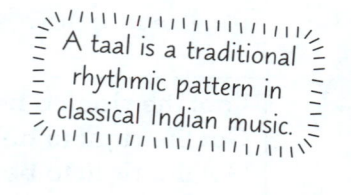

a) Write down an example of personification from the poem. Why do you think the poet has used this technique?

....

....

....

b) The poet uses lots of verbs in the third stanza. What is the effect of this?

....

c) Why do you think the poet uses very little punctuation in the poem? Explain your answer.

....

....

d) Underline all the references to circles in the poem. Why do you think the poet includes lots of references to circles? Explain your answer.

NOW TRY THIS Go back to the start of this section and have another read through the poems. Make a note of any that you particularly liked. Then, write a short paragraph about the poem you liked the most, explaining why it is your favourite. Was it its language, voice, message or something else entirely?

Section 4: Reading — Poetry © Not to be photocopied

Section 5: Reading — Comparing Texts

Shall I compare ~~thee~~ one text to ~~a summer's day~~ another text? Absolutely! The single most important thing to remember when comparing texts is to look at similarities AND differences. Oh, and make sure you back up your points with evidence and explanations too. OK that was two things... but they're both just as important.

Before you Start

1. The two texts below are about a prank that had unexpected consequences.

   A

   <u>Monday 8th July</u>
   I can't believe Victor stole my scooter and left it in the woods. He'll be as sorry as a cat in a bath once I'm done with him.

   <u>Tuesday 9th July</u>
   I have devised the most inventive prank to get my revenge. Edgar, our Great Dane, has been disguised as a rather convincing lion with the help of a fake mane. I've also installed a device in his collar to make it sound like he's roaring. I'll wait until Victor is walking down our street, then I'll let Edgar out of the house.

   <u>Wednesday 10th July</u>
   Things may have got slightly out of hand.

   B

   LION ON THE LOOSE!

   On Tuesday 9th July, Redhaven residents were perplexed and petrified to see a young male lion run through a residential area, roar at a group of teenagers and then disappear into the local woodland.

   "I was shaking like a leaf when I saw it", claimed one teen.

   It is thought that the lion may have been allowed to escape from the local safari park, though they have not yet commented on this alarming accusation.

   Residents are advised to stay in their homes with their doors locked. Any sightings of the lion must be reported to the Royal Organisation for Animal Recapture to ensure both the lion's safety and their own.

   a) i) Which of the following language techniques is used in both texts?

   metaphor ☐   simile ☐   alliteration ☐   repetition ☐

   ii) Write down an example of this technique from each text.

   ....

   ....

   b) i) How would you describe the tone of Text A? Use evidence to support your answer.

   ....

   ....

   ....

   ....

   ii) How is the tone in Text B different to the tone in Text A? Explain your answer.

   c) Write down two more differences between Text A and Text B.

Comparing Texts

Now let's put the skills you've just practised to the test. I've selected three fabulous texts for you to read and given you a couple of pages of questions to get you thinking about how they are similar or different. Enjoy!

An adapted extract from *The Canterville Ghost* by Oscar Wilde

"My *dear* sir," said Mr. Otis, "I really must insist on your oiling those chains, and have brought you for that purpose a small bottle of the Tammany Rising Sun Lubricator. It is said to be highly effective upon one application, and there are several testimonials to that effect on the wrapper from some of our most eminent clergymen. I shall leave it here for you by the bedroom candles, and will be happy to supply you with more should you require it." With these words the United States Minister laid the bottle down on a marble table, and, closing his door, retired to rest.

For a moment the Canterville ghost stood quite motionless in natural indignation; then, dashing the bottle violently upon the polished floor, he fled down the corridor, uttering hollow groans, and emitting a ghastly green light. Just, however, as he reached the top of the great oak staircase, a door was flung open, two little white-robed figures appeared, and a large pillow whizzed past his head! There was evidently no time to be lost, so, hastily adopting the Fourth Dimension of Space as a means of escape, he vanished through the panelled walls, and the house became quite quiet.

On reaching a small secret chamber in the left wing, he leaned up against a moonbeam to recover his breath, and began to try and realise his position.

Never, in a brilliant and uninterrupted career of three hundred years, had he been so grossly insulted. He thought of the Dowager Duchess, whom he had frightened into a fit as she stood before the glass in her lace and diamonds; of the four housemaids, who had gone off into hysterics when he merely grinned at them through the curtains of one of the spare bedrooms; of the rector of the parish, whose candle he had blown out as he was coming late one night from the library, and who had been under the care of Sir William Gull ever since, as a constant sufferer of nervous disorders; and of old Madame de Tremouillac, who, having wakened up one morning early and seen a skeleton seated in an armchair by the fire reading her diary, had been confined to her bed for six weeks with an attack of brain fever, and, on her recovery, had turned to the Church.

An extract from a short story called *The Intruder* (continued on the next page)

"I know you're there!" shouted Bushra defiantly into the inky blackness, her voice reverberating off the cold stone walls. She was committed to confronting whatever lurked in the corridor. She had grown accustomed to the odd noises that this relic of a mansion made as it settled down for the night: creaking floorboards overhead, wind whistling under doors and the occasional tap on the window from the oak trees outside. But tonight, the noises were different. Someone or something was trespassing.

Suddenly, an icy breeze whipped through Bushra's long hair, as if somebody had opened the large window behind her. Bushra quickly spun around to face the intruder, her arms raised defensively, but the heavy iron latches were still secure. Uneasiness washed over her like a stormy wave and cold beads of sweat rolled down her back like hailstones. However, Bushra refused to acknowledge them. *Mind over matter*, she thought. There was always a reasonable and logical explanation for everything.

Comparing Texts

"Show yourself!" Bushra commanded with the authority of an army general. Her eyes danced around every corner of the room, desperately trying to spot the slightest sign of movement. But the still silence persisted. She exhaled deeply before turning around to leave the room. Had she not already been on edge, she may have missed the almost imperceptible figure of a girl cowering against the tapestry in front of her. She must have been about eight or nine years old, though this was only a guess, as the girl had covered her face with her pale, trembling hands. Her hair was in two pigtails tied neatly with ribbons and she wore an old-fashioned, floral dress with an apron.

Bushra's defensive demeanour softened slightly — this was hardly the formidable threat she had been expecting. She crouched down in front of the girl and moved to put a reassuring hand on her shoulder. However, where her hand should have met the resistance of flesh and bone, she felt a biting chill creep through her body as the tips of her fingers made contact with the rough embroidery of the tapestry. On closer inspection, she also realised that the pattern on the girl's dress wasn't a pattern at all: they were the flowers on the tapestry behind her. Bushra sharply withdrew her hand from the cold nothingness and stared wide-eyed at the ghostly girl peeking through her shaking hands. Bushra rubbed her eyes with her fists, hoping that she was just imagining things, but the ghostly girl remained.

"P-p-please," begged the girl with the shrill resonance of a spectral voice, "I mean you no harm."

An extract from an article called *Haunted Holidays*

A Phantom in the Lake District

Some holidaymakers flee at the mere mention of ghosts, but others believe such sightings add to a location's appeal. Perhaps that's why places like Muncaster Castle are so popular with tourists.

Muncaster Castle is a 13th-century castle located near the village of Ravenglass, West Cumbria. This impressive structure has been owned by the Pennington family for as many as 900 years. But it is their 16th-century jester, Thomas Skelton or 'Tom the Fool', who steals the show as he is thought to be the culprit behind some of the ghostly goings-on.

It is thought that Skelton died around 1600, and his ghost continues to be blamed for the pranks that torment unsuspecting visitors. This is hardly surprising as he is believed to be the origin of the word 'tomfoolery'.

Most of the castle's hauntings appear to be focused around one particular place — the Tapestry Room. Here, visitors have claimed to feel an inexplicable chill come over them and to have heard footsteps in the corridor outside the room. However, the most mysterious assertion of all comes from those who have dared stay the night in the Tapestry Room. Apparently, the door handle has turned of its own accord and the door has creepily creaked open like a predator's jaws to reveal nothing but an empty corridor.

It is somewhat unfair to blame all of these supernatural shenanigans on Skelton, though. Other strange happenings have been attributed to Margaret Pennington, a sickly girl who died whilst staying at the castle. This would better explain the sound of crying that can sometimes be heard near the window in one room, and also the voice of a woman who appears to sing a comforting melody to a sick child.

Whether you believe these tales or discount them as codswallop, a visit to Muncaster Castle is sure to awe and amuse.

Comparing Texts

1. a) What is the main purpose of *Haunted Holidays*? Circle one.

to entertain   to explain   to inform   to argue

b) Does *The Canterville Ghost* have the same purpose as *Haunted Holidays*? Explain your answer.

....

....

2. What effect do the similes below have on the reader? Explain your answer.

The Intruder	**Haunted Holidays**
"Uneasiness washed over her like a stormy wave"	"creepily creaked open like a predator's jaws"

....

....

....

3. a) What technique is used in *The Intruder* and *Haunted Holidays* to describe a ghostly presence? Tick one box.

metaphor ☐   sensory language ☐   persuasive language ☐   onomatopoeia ☐

b) Write down an example of this technique from each text.

....

....

4. Give one way that the ghost from *The Canterville Ghost* is similar to Tom the Fool's ghost in *Haunted Holidays*. Give evidence from each text to support your answer.

....

....

....

Comparing Texts

5. Compare the layout of *The Canterville Ghost* and *Haunted Holidays*.

....

....

....

6. Give one way that the setting in *Haunted Holidays* is similar to the setting in *The Intruder*. Give evidence from both texts to support your answer.

....

....

....

....

7. a) Write down one word to describe the Canterville ghost's personality.

....

b) Give an example from the text to explain your choice.

....

....

c) Compare your impression of the Canterville ghost with your impression of the ghostly girl in *The Intruder*. Give evidence from the texts in your answer.

8. Compare the mood created in *The Canterville Ghost* and *The Intruder*. Use details from the texts to support your answer.

9. Re-read *The Intruder* and *Haunted Holidays*. Write two paragraphs comparing the extracts. Use quotations to back up your points.

Remember to look at both similarities and differences when comparing.

NOW TRY THIS: Choose one of the extracts on p.40-41 and pick a character from it. Write a diary entry that describes the events in the extract from your chosen character's perspective. Make sure you use an appropriate tone, structure and layout, and try to include lots of interesting vocabulary.

Section 6: Reading Review

Now that you've worked your way through the reading part of this book, it's time to test your skills. The adapted extract below is from *Animal Farm* by George Orwell. In *Animal Farm*, some animals rebel against their neglectful human farmer and take control of their farm. At this point in the story, some animals have just been killed by those in charge after having confessed to committing crimes.

> The animals huddled about Clover, not speaking. The knoll where they were lying gave them a wide prospect across the countryside. Most of Animal Farm was within their view — the long pasture stretching down to the main road, the hayfield, the spinney, the drinking pool, the ploughed fields where the young wheat was thick and green, and the red roofs of the farm buildings with the smoke curling from the chimneys. It was a clear spring evening. The grass and the bursting hedges were gilded by the level rays of the sun. Never had the farm — and with a kind of surprise they remembered that it was their own farm, every inch of it their own property — appeared to the animals so desirable a place.
>
> As Clover looked down the hillside, her eyes filled with tears. If she could have spoken her thoughts, it would have been to say that this was not what they had aimed at when they had set themselves years ago to work for the overthrow of the human race. These scenes of terror and slaughter were not what they had looked forward to on that night when old Major first stirred them to rebellion. If she herself had had any picture of the future, it had been of a society of animals set free from hunger and the whip, all equal, each working according to his capacity, the strong protecting the weak, as she had protected the lost brood of ducklings with her foreleg on the night of Major's speech.
>
> Instead — she did not know why — they had come to a time when no one dared speak his mind, when fierce, growling dogs roamed everywhere, and when you had to watch your comrades torn to pieces after confessing to shocking crimes.
>
> There was no thought of rebellion or disobedience in her mind. She knew that even as things were, they were far better off than they had been in the days of Jones, and that before all else it was necessary to prevent the return of the human beings. Whatever happened, she would remain faithful, work hard, carry out the orders that were given to her, and accept the leadership of Napoleon.
>
> But still, it was not for this that she and all the other animals had hoped and toiled.

1. Write out a description from the extract that suggests the farm is doing well.

....

1 mark

2. Find and copy some emotive language that describes the animals' current situation.

....

1 mark

3. How does Clover feels when she looks at the farm? How can you tell?

....

....

2 marks

4. What was the main aim of the animals' rebellion?

....

1 mark

5. a) Summarise the outcome that Clover expected from the rebellion.

....

....

....

2 marks

b) Have the animals achieved this outcome? Give two reasons for your answer.

....

....

....

....

3 marks

6. Why do you think the animals are "not speaking" in this extract? Explain your answer using details from the extract.

2 marks

7. Describe Clover's change in attitude from the start of the rebellion to now. Use details from the extract to support your answer.

4 marks

© Not to be photocopied

Section 6: Reading Review

Reading Review

This extract is from the play *Face* by Benjamin Zephaniah. Martin was in a car crash which left his face badly scarred. When in hospital, he met a boy called Anthony who also has facial disfigurements.

FORM TUTOR	Martin, is that you? I'm glad I found you in.
PRESENT MARTIN	My mum and dad aren't here.
FORM TUTOR	That's okay — I know it seems odd, your form teacher on your doorstep, but I thought perhaps we should talk about what you want to do about returning.
PRESENT MARTIN	Returning?
FORM TUTOR	How long you want to leave it. We understand that you may not feel ready to 'hit the ground running' at the start of term, so perhaps you'd like work sent home until you feel more — prepared, when things have calmed down a little, when the other students have had a chance to get used to — the new situation.
NARRATIVE MARTIN	It was *almost* sweet — and I was so tempted to say I needed the rest of term off, to hide in my room and get on with things in secret, to turn my face away. But then I thought, 'What would Anthony do?'
ANTHONY	(*walking through, unobserved*) People will stare — they will do that for the rest of your life.
NARRATIVE MARTIN	How would he deal with this?
ANTHONY	The problem is with them, not with you.
NARRATIVE MARTIN	What would he tell them all?
ANTHONY	You have to hang in there. (*exits*)
NARRATIVE MARTIN	And it was suddenly very clear.
PRESENT MARTIN	(*opens door wide*) Term starts on Monday, yes?
FORM TUTOR	(*surprised*) Yes, that's right.
PRESENT MARTIN	Then I'd best be there, I guess.
FORM TUTOR	Martin, do you think that's — ?
PRESENT MARTIN	(*sharply, indignantly*) Yes, I do. I'm not going to hide. And I'm not going to wait until you've had a chance to do a nice assembly on me and what's happened. I'm not ashamed. I didn't do anything wrong, I just made a mistake, and I'm paying for it enough as it is, thank you very much. My brain still works — it's just the face that's changed and the sooner people get used to that, the better.
FORM TUTOR	Perhaps your parents might like to —
PRESENT MARTIN	You ask them if you want, but they know that when I've made up my mind, that's it.
FORM TUTOR	It may be hard for you at first.
PRESENT MARTIN	*Whenever* I come back it will be hard. Next Monday or the Monday after that, or the one after that. There has to be a first day — I'd I rather get it over and done with.
FORM TUTOR	If you're sure.
PRESENT MARTIN	I'm sure (*softening a little*) but thanks for asking, anyway. See you then.
FORM TUTOR	Good luck, Martin.

'Present Martin' and 'Narrative Martin' are the same person, but they're each looking at events from a different point in time.

1. Why has Martin's form tutor come to his house?

   ....

   ☐ 1 mark

2. Read the form tutor's lines starting "How long" and ending "new situation". How do you think the actor playing the form tutor should say these lines? Explain your answer.

   ....

   ....

   ☐ 2 marks

3. Write down the stage direction that shows that Martin is open to returning to school.

   ....

   ☐ 1 mark

4. Give two reasons why Martin wants to return to school on Monday.

   ....

   ....

   ....

   ☐ 2 marks

5. Briefly explain the role of Anthony in this extract.

   ....

   ....

   ....

   ☐ 2 marks

6. Why do you think the form tutor wishes Martin "Good luck"? Explain your answer.

   ....

   ....

   ....

   ☐ 2 marks

7. Why do you think the author chose to include Narrative Martin in the play? Use details from the text to support your answer.

   ☐ 2 marks

8. What impression do you get of Martin as a character? Explain your answer using details from the extract.

   ☐ 6 marks

© Not to be photocopied   Section 6: Reading Review

Reading Review

The text below is a book review from a newspaper. Read the text, then have a go at the questions. Keep referring back to the review when you are writing your answers.

Someone, No one: A Flight of Fantasy

As the old saying goes, "don't judge a book by its cover"; however, in the case of Theresa Milna's *Someone, No one*, I couldn't resist.

The Moment of Discovery

Picture the scene. I stroll through my local bookshop, eyes flickering restlessly over the books which are strewn across long tables like colourful confetti. I am hungry — ravenous — for my next read and I hunt my prey like a wolf with long, swooping glances, reading and rejecting titles in an instant. But then — I see it. The small, black volume sits unassumingly between two brightly coloured books which clamour for attention. I ignore them and eagerly dive for the slim, mysterious novel. *Someone, No one*, the title reads in delicate lettering. I have found my next read.

Taking Flight

It was with high expectations that I pried open the pages later that day — and I was not disappointed. Milna launches the reader into a intoxicating world of magic, mystery and intrigue, right from the first sentence: "Once, I was someone; now, I am no one." Who could fail to be drawn in by this opening line? Milna's brilliant writing continued to surprise and thrill me throughout the novel, as she moved seamlessly between passages of vivid description and short, sharp chunks of dialogue with a confident, assured manner which it is rare to find in a first-time novelist.

Although I am not normally a fan of the fantasy genre, *Someone, No one* utterly captivated me through its subtle blend of the familiar world with the fantastical. Take the novel's main character, for instance. Estaa is a typical teenage girl who struggles to navigate school, friendships and her family — but she's got amazing magical powers. The plot also follows this pattern: although set in the sleepy suburbs, we soon come to realise that it's not exactly your average small town (unless your town is inhabited by feisty fairies, world-famous wizards and a power-hungry dragon, hunting greedily for its next innocent victim.)

My Top Four Fantasy Reads

1. *The Sorcerer's Secret*
   Wizards, a dragon and an evil villain: a classic choice.
2. *Hattie Jones: Witch*
   At once hilarious, sad and gripping: this book has it all.
3. *The Time We Lost*
   A heartbreaking romance, sprinkled with spells.
4. *Spellbinding*
   Poems which explore the magic of everyday life.

Some Bumps Along the Way

However, Milna's writing is not without imperfections. Although it was a joy to watch Estaa flourish from a timid, socially awkward teen into a strong, powerful young woman, many of the other characters failed to pack a punch and were largely forgettable. Moreover, though the plot rattled along at an exciting pace, at times I felt myself craving a moment to catch my breath. As this is a relatively short novel — only 150 pages — Milna could have fleshed out parts of the story more to help vary the book's pace. I certainly wouldn't have minded reading another twenty or thirty pages!

To Read or Not to Read

The simple answer is 'yes, absolutely'. Despite a few flaws, *Someone, No one* is a superbly readable novel which will make you laugh, cry and gasp, all in the same chapter. If you're still unsure, let me ask you some questions. Do you like fantasy novels? Then this is the book for you. Do you want to read beautiful, descriptive, gripping writing? Give this book a read. Do you simply enjoy a good book? Again, Milna's work ticks every box.

For once, this is a book that *can* be judged by its cover; the contents were as mysterious, interesting and beautiful as its exterior.

1. Why did the writer of the article choose to read *Someone, No one*?

   ....

   1 mark

2. In your own words, briefly summarise what *Someone, No one* is about.

   ....

   ....

   ....

   3 marks

3. a) Write down a simile from the section "The Moment of Discovery".

   ....

   1 mark

   b) Why do you think the writer used this simile?

   ....

   ....

   2 marks

4. Give two layout features from the review and explain why the writer used them.

   ....

   ....

   ....

   4 marks

5. a) What is the purpose of the section "To Read or Not to Read"?

   ....

   1 mark

   b) How does the writer use language to achieve this purpose? Give two examples from the text to support your answer.

   3 marks

6. Describe the tone of the review. What effect does the tone have on the reader?

   2 marks

7. Sum up the writer's opinion of *Someone, No one*, using evidence from the whole text.

   4 marks

8. Does the writer make you want to read the novel? Explain your answer.

   2 marks

© Not to be photocopied

Section 6: Reading Review

Reading Review

The extract below is from *Romeo and Juliet* by William Shakespeare. Read the extract carefully, then answer the questions on the next page.

BENVOLIO	Good morrow, cousin.
ROMEO	Is the day so young?
BENVOLIO	But new struck nine.
ROMEO	Ay me! Sad hours seem long. Was that my father that went hence* so fast?
BENVOLIO	It was. What sadness lengthens Romeo's hours?
ROMEO	Not having that, which, having, makes them short.
BENVOLIO	In love?
ROMEO	Out —
BENVOLIO	Of love?
ROMEO	Out of her favour where I am in love.
BENVOLIO	Alas that love so gentle in his view, Should be so tyrannous and rough in proof!
ROMEO	Alas, that love, whose view is muffled still, Should, without eyes, see pathways to his will! Where shall we dine? O me! What fray* was here? Yet tell me not, for I have heard it all. Here's much to do with hate, but more with love. Why, then, O brawling love, O loving hate, O anything of nothing first create! O heavy lightness, serious vanity, Misshapen chaos of well-seeming* forms! Feather of lead, bright smoke, cold fire, sick health! Still-waking sleep, that is not what it is! This love feel I, that feel no love in this. Dost* thou not laugh?
BENVOLIO	No, coz*, I rather weep.
ROMEO	Good heart, at what?
BENVOLIO	At thy good heart's oppression.
ROMEO	Why, such is love's transgression*. Griefs of mine own lie heavy in my breast, Which thou wilt propagate*, to have it pressed With more of thine; this love that thou hast shown Doth add more grief to too much of mine own.

Benvolio and Romeo are cousins. In this extract, Benvolio is trying to understand why Romeo has been acting differently recently.

*hence — from here
*fray — fight
*well-seeming — beautiful
*Dost — do
*coz — cousin
*transgression — crime
*propagate — make bigger

1. What time of day is it at the start of the extract?

   ....

   1 mark

2. a) How does Romeo feel at the start of the extract? Write down a quote that supports your answer.

   ....

   ....

   2 marks

   b) Why does Romeo feel this way? Use an example from the text to support your answer.

   ....

   ....

   2 marks

3. a) Romeo describes love as "Feather of lead, bright smoke, cold fire, sick health". What language technique is used in this line?

   ....

   1 mark

   b) What does this description suggest about love? Explain your answer.

   ....

   ....

   ....

   2 marks

4. Read from "No, coz, I rather weep" to "At thy good heart's oppression". Why is Benvolio upset in this part of the extract? Use the text to support your answer.

   ....

   ....

   ....

   2 marks

5. What impression do you get of Romeo from this extract? Explain your answer.

   2 marks

6. How does Shakespeare show that Romeo and Benvolio have a close relationship? Support your answer using details from the extract.

   4 marks

© Not to be photocopied — Section 6: Reading Review

Section 7: Writing — Non-Fiction Writing

BREAKING NEWS — it appears as though our student has made it through the Reading section and is now ready to commence their journey through none other than the Writing section. They'll start with some warm-up questions about non-fiction texts and then progress from there. It's sure to be a wild ride.

Before you Start

1. Number the sentences 1-3 so that they are in the most logical order.

    i) A simple way to relax and unwind from life is reading.

    ii) Modern life is increasingly fast-paced and busy.

    iii) It helps you to relax and could alleviate feelings of anxiety.

2. Read these opening sentences of non-fiction texts, then write what you think the purpose of each text is on the dotted lines.

    A The oldest pair of traditional socks was excavated in Egypt in the late 1800s. They date back to AD 250-420.

    ....

    B Keep your favourite socks in top-notch condition with our natural, gentle and eco-friendly fabric conditioner.

    ....

    C If your feet are cold, fluffy socks are normally the best option. Alternatively, you can layer two thinner pairs.

    ....

    D There is no doubt that the greatest crime against fashion is the abhorrent combination of socks and sandals.

    ....

3. Rewrite the sentences below so that they use more formal language.

    a) I can't come along to the Christmas do.

    ....

    b) You'll find loads of cool stuff in the museum.

    ....

    c) We shouldn't bother with that film — it's rubbish.

    ....

Planning

It does sound awfully tempting to just start writing without a plan, but trust me — it can get chaotic pretty quickly. Even if you just jot down a few notes to help structure your points, your writing will thank you.

1. The two plans below are for an essay about your favourite book or film.

   A I'll talk about my favourite film.
   Lots of action and easy to understand.
   Everybody should watch it at some point in their lives.
   They're releasing a sequel soon and I'm going to the cinema to watch it.
   The main character is really cool and has lots of friends. I really liked him.

   B Intro — Introduce book and the author.
   1) Protagonist is from Ghana (like me).
   2) Set in Italy (my favourite country) — describes sights really well.
   3) Aimed at a younger audience but doesn't sound childish.
   Conclusion — A relatable book that covers a lot of my interests and isn't patronising.

   a) Which is the better plan? Explain your answer.

   ....

   ....

   b) Rewrite the plan you didn't choose in part a) to improve it.

2. Below are three topics for a letter to your school council.

   | You want the school to arrange donations to a local food bank. | You want to study a wider range of cultures in school. | You want the cafeteria to offer multiple vegetarian and vegan options. |

   a) Choose one of the topics above, then use the table below to write a brief plan for the letter.

Introduction	
Point 1	
Point 2	
Point 3	
Conclusion	

   b) Use your plan from part a) to write your letter.

NOW TRY THIS — Use the good plan from Question 1 to help you plan an essay about your favourite book or film. Jot down three reasons why you like it and any details you want to include in the introduction and conclusion. Then write your essay in full, starting a new paragraph for each point in your plan.

Structure

It's like my dear old granny used to say: "Make sure you write an engaging introduction, a well-structured middle and a clear conclusion in your non-fiction texts." Not very catchy I'll grant you, but she wasn't wrong.

1. Here are two introductions to an essay. Which one do you think is better? Explain why.

A Bees are striped insects with wings. Some people think of them as cute, furry little flying things but I think they're a nuisance. I stood on a bee once when I was little and it stung me on the foot — what's cute about that?

B Pollinators, such as bees, don't just pollinate our flowers — they play a vital role in producing the UK's food. Without bees, the UK would almost certainly experience food shortages, affecting the lives of many people.

....

....

2. The following points have been taken from an essay about yoga.

○ However, there is more to yoga than just exercise. By connecting movement to breath, we clear our minds of negative thoughts, benefiting our mental health.

○ First and foremost, yoga is a form of exercise. It makes us stronger, improves our flexibility and raises our heart rate. These all improve our general physical wellbeing.

○ These physical and mental benefits mean yoga has surged in popularity in recent years, with many places offering classes. It's a great way to integrate yourself into a community.

a) Number the points 1-3 based on the order they should come in the text.

b) Tick the introductory sentence that you think is the most engaging for this text.

   i) This essay will talk about yoga, a type of exercise with lots of benefits. ☐

   ii) Ever thought that yoga just isn't for you? This essay will challenge that mindset. ☐

   iii) I've been told I have to write an essay about yoga so here it is. ☐

c) Use the points and introductory sentence above to write a clear conclusion to this text.

....

....

....

....

Structure

3. The sentences in this paragraph have been jumbled up. Rewrite it in a more logical order.

> However, evidence shows that a large percentage of the sun's damaging rays can penetrate clouds. This shows just how vital it is to protect your skin with suncream every day, regardless of the weather. Many people wrongly assume that they can get away with not wearing suncream on cloudy days.

4. Read the first part of a paragraph in the box below.

> If the thought of setting your alarm clock for 5.30am fills you with dread, you're not alone. Many of us find it difficult to leave the cosy comfort of our warm beds, but those who do so before dawn may experience greater success in their work and home lives.

a) Tick the sentence that would continue this paragraph in the best way.

i) My grandad always got up early and he lived to be 102 years old. ☐

ii) However, if getting up early means that you're constantly tired, it's pointless. ☐

iii) Recent studies have shown that early risers are more productive and organised. ☐

b) Then write a final sentence to complete the paragraph.

5. Choose one of the statements below and write a paragraph to agree or disagree with it. Make sure your paragraph has a clear, logical structure.

> People shouldn't use their phones when sat at the dinner table.

> Invisibility would be the best superpower.

> Dogs make better pets than cats.

6. Imagine that you're writing an article convincing people to try your favourite hobby.

a) Write three key points that you would include to convince people to try your hobby.

....

....

....

b) Now write your article. Make sure it has an engaging introduction and a clear conclusion.

Quoting

Using quotes is a brilliant way to back up your points with evidence. Make sure you weave quotes into your writing rather than stating them in separate sentences — it'll help your writing flow more naturally.

1. Write down whether each statement below about using quotes is true or false.

   a) Don't bother copying quotes word-for-word — it's a waste of time. ....

   b) A longer quote is always better than a shorter quote. ....

   c) Use quotation marks at the start and end of every quote. ....

   d) You should always explain how a quote supports your point. ....

2. Below is an extract from a story and two extracts from essays about it.

   > My mind was a whirlpool. Everything that I had believed about myself — my abilities and how people would react to them — it was all wrong. These strange powers that I had kept hidden for so long were now being celebrated.

   A The narrator likens their mind to "a whirlpool", which clearly illustrates the tumultuous nature of their thoughts. This metaphor emphasises how their discovery has disrupted everything that they previously believed about their "strange powers".

   B The narrator uses a metaphor by saying that their mind is a whirlpool, which represents the sheer confusion that they are experiencing. It highlights that the effect of learning the true nature of their "special powers" is extremely unsettling.

   Which essay extract has used quotes incorrectly? Explain your answer.

   ....
   ....
   ....

3. Decide which two quotes on the right are relevant to the extract below, then rewrite the extract to insert the relevant quotes.

   You don't need to use the whole quotes — you can just use parts if it will make the paragraph flow better.

   > The author describes the abandoned laboratory using sensory language. This language engages the reader's senses, and helps them to better imagine what the laboratory is like after being vacant for so long.

   a) "The room hummed with crowded conversations."

   b) "the acrid smell of old experiments"

   c) "The cobwebs tickled my legs as I walked."

Writing Essays

I know this page probably sounds a bit scary but don't worry — essays really aren't as bad as they sound. Just try to think of them as answers to a question. Write formally and clearly and you'll be absolutely fine.

1. Briefly plan out three main points for each essay question below.

   > Explain the advantages and disadvantages of the council building more sports facilities in your area.

   > Argue in favour of opening a theme park on the outskirts of your hometown.

   > Argue against the decision to stop selling popcorn and fizzy drinks at the cinema.

   > Explain why students shouldn't have to do homework during the school holidays.

2. This is part of a plan for an essay about public transport.

   > Introduction — Purpose of the essay and basic outline of what it will cover
   > Point 1 — One advantage of using public transport, e.g. less pollution
   > Point 2 — One disadvantage of using public transport, e.g. train and bus delays
   > Point 3 — Personal opinion about public transport

   a) Write an essay question that fits the essay plan above.

   ....

   b) List two other advantages that you could add as new points after Point 1.

   ....
   ....

   c) List two other disadvantages that you could add as new points after Point 2.

   ....
   ....

   d) Briefly summarise what your conclusion to the essay would say.

   e) Use the plan and your answers above to write out the essay to your question in part a).

Now Try This: Now it's time to have a go at writing an essay from scratch. Choose one of the essay plans from Question 1. Plan what you want to say in your introduction and conclusion, then expand your plan to write the essay out in full. Make sure you use a clear structure for your main paragraphs.

Formal and Informal Language

Formal language is more serious and professional, so it's normally saved for when you're writing to people you don't know. You can use chattier, informal language if you're writing to somebody you know well.

1. Some non-fiction texts require formal language, while others require informal language. Write three examples of each in the table. Use the example below to get you started.

Informal	Formal
A diary entry about your holiday last year.	

2. Rewrite the sentences below so that they use formal language.

   a) She was gutted that she couldn't meet her mate for a cuppa.

   ....

   b) I think I'd be great at the job you've popped on your website.

   ....

   c) We were pretty peckish so we bought some grub.

   ....

3. The box below contains some formal words. Write a paragraph for a formal letter that uses all of the words in the box.

   | assistance | enquire | occupation | demonstrate |
   | incorrect | however | verify | considerable |

4. Imagine you have just received a letter from your friend about what they did during the summer holidays. Write a reply using informal language.

Writing to Inform, Explain and Advise

Most of the non-fiction texts you'll come across will either inform, explain or advise. Whether you want to provide information, explain something or offer advice, it's important to know what each purpose requires.

1. Write 'A' (Advise), 'I' (Inform) or 'E' (Explain) in the boxes to show whether each feature should be used to advise, inform or explain.

   Uses examples and evidence to help someone understand ☐

   Gives suggestions with polite language rather than commands ☐

   Usually assumes the reader knows nothing about the topic ☐

   Gives the reader lots of facts, presented in an engaging way ☐

   Often addresses the reader with second-person pronouns ☐

   Provides clear, balanced information about a certain topic ☐

2. Write a sentence explaining why each of the statements below is a good idea. Make sure you use the features of writing to explain that you identified in Question 1.

   a) You should eat five portions of fruit and vegetables a day.

   b) Everyone should aim to do some volunteering when they can.

   c) You should avoid going on holiday during term time.

3. Use the facts below to write a short informative paragraph about the many uses of beetroot.

   Just call me un-beet-able.

   | Beetroots are very good for you — they're full of vitamins and minerals. | The sweetness of beetroots makes them an ideal baking ingredient. | Their potent pink juice can be used as a natural dye. |

   ....

   ....

   ....

   ....

Writing to Inform, Explain and Advise

4. The text below is giving advice about going to the beach.

> You must never go to the beach when it is rainy or windy. It is better to just stay dry inside and wait for the weather to improve. However, if you absolutely insist on not heeding my warning, make sure you wear as many waterproofs as possible. And don't even think about not wearing your wellies — you (and your socks) will regret it.

a) Looking back at your answers to Question 1, what is the problem with this advice text? Explain your answer.

....
....
....

b) Rewrite the text to fix the problem you mentioned in part a).

5. a) Write a few sentences about your hometown for each of the purposes below.

i) A fact-file about your hometown and the surrounding area

....
....
....

ii) A leaflet advising people on the best things to do in your hometown

....
....
....

b) Write an article for a travel website explaining how you feel about your hometown. Make sure you include each of the features listed below:

i) A description of your hometown

ii) Some facts about your hometown, e.g. where it is, how many people live there

iii) Reasons why you like or dislike your hometown

NOW TRY THIS — You need to give lots of facts when you're writing a text to inform. Think about an animal that you find impressive, then do some research online and find at least six interesting facts about it. Once you've gathered your facts, use them to write an information leaflet about this animal.

Writing to Persuade and Argue

There are lots of different techniques that you can use when writing to persuade and argue, but I'm sure I won't need to use any of them to persuade you to answer all the questions on the following two pages.

1. Write down whether each statement below is true or false.

   a) When writing to argue, only talk about how other opinions are wrong. ....

   b) Writing to persuade is about encouraging the reader to do something. ....

   c) You need to give clear and convincing reasons for both purposes. ....

2. Rewrite the sentences below to use lists of three.

   > A list of three is a persuasive technique that uses three adjectives instead of one to describe something.

   a) I was horrified at the state of the hotel room.

   ....

   b) It is shameful that we were treated in this way.

   ....

   c) This role would suit a hard-working individual like me.

   ....

3. Match each of the following techniques to a sentence from the text by writing **A-E** in the boxes provided. Use each option once.

   A) question   B) exaggeration   C) 'list of three'   D) 'we' and 'us'   E) counter-argument

   > I think we can all agree that the summer holidays are too long for us students. Some believe that the long break is beneficial, but I believe they are mistaken — recent research shows that it can actually negatively impact our learning. Why should we spend a whole year working our socks off only to be hindered the following year by our holiday? I personally find the novelty of the break soon wears off and I become bored, frustrated and lonely in a matter of days. I'm sure millions of students are in agreement with me, so I propose that we cut three weeks from the summer holidays and make half term longer instead.

4. Rewrite the persuasive text below so that it exaggerates the positive points about the resort.

   > We think you'll probably like our resort. We have some nice facilities. The swimming pool was built a few years ago and it's still in fairly good condition. We received a couple of nice reviews last year about our food too. There's a good chance that you'll enjoy your holiday if you stay with us this summer. We hope to see you soon.

© Not to be photocopied

Section 7: Writing — Non-Fiction Writing

Writing to Persuade and Argue

5. The sentences below are from texts arguing for or against an issue.

Signing a petition might not make a big difference. ☐

Robots should probably be used to do household chores. ☐

All types of pollution negatively impact our fragile planet. ☐

a) Tick the sentence that has the most convincing argument. Explain your answer below.

....

....

b) Rewrite the sentences you didn't choose in part a) so that they present more convincing arguments.

6. For each statement below, write a short paragraph which argues in favour of the statement.

a) It's wrong that some students get away with bullying others.

b) People deserve to have more time to do the things they enjoy.

7. a) The passage below is about how to ensure your persuasive writing doesn't offend anyone. Use the words in the box to fill in the gaps in the passage.

| impersonal   support   attack   involve   criticisms   positive |

Persuasive writing should not directly .... your opponents. Instead, any

.... should be .... and general. However, you should

refer to "we" or "you" when making .... points, as this will help to

.... the reader and encourage them to .... you.

b) Rewrite the extract below, using the techniques from the passage above to improve it.

> If you think that this problem doesn't concern you then you're a fool. How can you just sit idly and let the people around you suffer? Are you really that cruel? Ignoring a problem does not make it go away. People must unite to solve this problem with their compassion. This will triumph over your ignorance.

NOW TRY THIS: To write a convincing argument, you need to be able to understand both sides. Have another look at Question 3 on p.61, then write down three points for an argument that is in favour of long summer holidays for students. Try to use a variety of techniques from p.61-62 in your writing.

Section 8: Writing — Fiction Writing

Once upon a time, there was an incredibly talented individual whose only goal in life was to selflessly share their literary wisdom with the students of the world so that they could write the most incredible pieces of fiction. Okay, I might be exaggerating a teensy bit, but I still think you'll find these pages rather useful.

Before you Start

1. Which of the following features might you find in a good story? Tick all that apply.

   a) An opening sentence that grips the audience ☐

   b) Short chapters that interrupt the flow of the story ☐

   c) Exciting or interesting developments in the plot ☐

   d) An ending that contradicts what happens in the story ☐

   e) A loose end that leaves the audience wanting more ☐

   I'm just tidying up your loose ends...

2. Match each setting description to the genre it belongs in.

   'Genre' is just another word for 'category', e.g. romance or comedy.

   A The absence of birdsong left an eerie silence among the trees. Every footstep was amplified, and I had the unnerving sensation that someone was watching me.

   fairy tale

   B The escape pod was a mass of switches. Any label had faded long ago and the whirring machinery made it almost impossible for us to hear ourselves think.

   horror

   C At the top of the mountain stood a magnificent castle. Each turret was perfectly formed, its windows looking out onto the sleepy village under its protection.

   science fiction

3. Rewrite each description to show that the character is feeling the emotion in brackets.

   a) He stood against the wall and looked around the corner. (scared)

   ....

   ....

   b) She sat down at her desk and typed out the letter. (bored)

   ....

   ....

Planning

There's no place for waffle in your writing — it can confuse the reader or make them lose interest. Planning before you start will give you a well-thought-out story so that you can save the waffles for breakfast. Yum.

1. Tick the option that best describes what you should do when planning a story.

  a) Don't plan the opening line — you can usually use the same one. ☐

  b) Let the story unfold as you write, so don't plan the middle too much. ☐

  c) Plan your ending so you know what you're aiming towards. ☐

2. The plan below is for a short story.

> - Write about when my dog Buddy escaped — pretend he went on an adventure.
> - Happy ending — he comes back home at the end.
> - Reason for his escape — he ran through the hole in the fence to chase a squirrel.
> - Or he could be captured and has to defeat the dognappers before he can go home.
> - Or the squirrel he chases talks to him — Buddy needs to go on a quest to save the acorns...

  a) Why isn't this a very good plan?

  ....

  ....

  b) How do you think this plan could be improved? Give two suggestions.

  ....

  ....

  c) Write a new plan that includes the changes you suggested in part b).

3. The plan for the short story below is missing some plot points. Add some more plot points and some ideas for an opening line and a satisfying ending to the plan.

> - A teenager asks for help to stop the bullies in their school.
> - A spectral figure grants their wish by giving them special powers.
> - The powers must only be used with righteous intent. If used maliciously or selfishly, the powers will disappear.

Now Try This: Pssssst! I don't mean to alarm you but, if you've worked through the questions on this page, you're now the proud owner of two rather lovely plans. And I think they're up to the challenge. Try writing out one of the stories, aiming to write at least a paragraph for each point in your plan.

Section 8: Writing — Fiction Writing

Structure

Giving your story structure is a little like having a skeleton in your body — without one you'd be a messy blob on the floor. Your skeleton supports your body, just as a clear structure will support your story.

1. a) Which of the following describes a flashback? Tick one option.

   A part of a story that takes the reader back to past events. ☐

   A part of a story that hints to the reader about future events. ☐

   A moment where the main character reflects on their past. ☐

   b) Explain how you could use a flashback to make a story more interesting for the reader.

   ....

   ....

   ....

   ....

2. The plot points in this story have been jumbled up.

   ○ While they are out sailing, the light blue sky turns an ominous black and the wind picks up. A terrible storm is coming.

   ○ A family are on holiday on a tropical island. The air is balmy and the sun is warm. They think it is the perfect day to go sailing.

   ○ The family wash up on shore where they are met by a small community. They aid the family and provide them with food and shelter from the storm.

   ○ In an attempt to steer away from the storm, they crash into a reef. The boat starts sinking but they manage to steer it towards the coast of a small island.

   ○ During their stay, the family learn that the community is struggling to survive because a sacred artefact has been stolen. The family agree to find the artefact and return it to its rightful place.

   a) Number the parts of the story 1-5 so that they follow a sensible structure.

   b) Write three more plot points that develop the plot in an exciting way for the reader.

> **NOW TRY THIS** — Try writing out the story from Question 2 in full. Use the plot points from part a) (in the right order of course) and your points from part b) to form the basis of your plan. This will help you structure your story and should make it easier for you to keep track of what you want to happen and when.

Section 8: Writing — Fiction Writing

Building Character

Building character doesn't mean waltzing into the wilderness and trying to survive by yourself for a week — it's about using the actions and appearance of your characters to reflect who they are in their story.

1. What does each sentence tell you about the character whose name is in **bold**?

    a) **Natalie** sniggered as she threw the tennis ball at her unsuspecting brother.

    ....

    ....

    b) "**Raheem** is like a ray of sunshine on a cloudy day," said Joanna.

    ....

    ....

2. Read the passage below, then answer the questions.

    > Laura thrived when she was helping someone or something in need. No problem was too difficult to solve. Even if there was no obvious solution to the problem, she would always be there with a comforting word. Unless your dilemma involved animals, in which case she'd ignore you completely.

    a) Underline the sentence that doesn't fit with the rest of the character description.

    b) Explain why this doesn't fit the rest of the description.

    ....

    ....

    c) Replace this sentence with a new one that fits the rest of the description.

3. Write a paragraph to show the personality of each of the characters below. Make sure you use their actions and their appearance to help describe them.

Section 8: Writing — Fiction Writing

Building Setting

First you grab some bricks, then you mix some cement and then... Wait, that's not how you build setting? Oh... this page must be about developing the location where your fiction text takes place instead. Gotcha.

1. Rewrite this setting description to make it more suitable for each story below.

   > Tall trees stretched high into the air, blocking most of the light. The narrow path wound its way deep into the forest, eventually widening at a small clearing. At the edge of the clearing there was an old cottage.

   a) A horror story set in a remote forest

   b) A fairy tale set in a magical kingdom

2. Below are some settings with different atmospheres. Write a paragraph to describe each setting, making sure you create the atmosphere mentioned for each one.

   > Setting: an abandoned factory
   > Atmosphere: eerie

   > Setting: a football stadium
   > Atmosphere: joyful

   > Setting: a birthday party
   > Atmosphere: dull

   > Setting: a singing contest
   > Atmosphere: tense

3. The text below outlines the plot of an adventure story.

   Use figurative language to help your setting descriptions come alive.

   > It's midwinter, but there's not a flake of snow in sight. Antarctica is melting, so the colony elects a team of plucky penguins to seek an audience with the Snow God. Only then can the cold return.

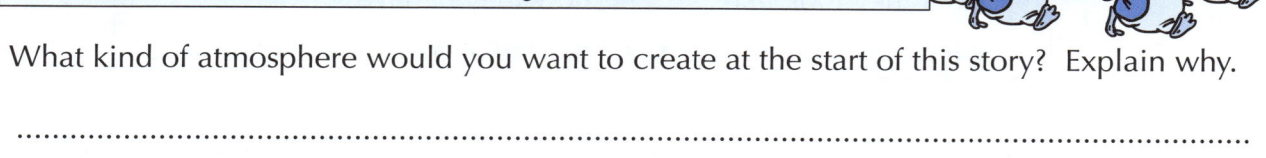

   a) What kind of atmosphere would you want to create at the start of this story? Explain why.

   ....

   ....

   b) How would you use the setting to help you create this atmosphere?

   ....

   ....

   ....

   c) Using your answers from a) and b), write a paragraph of the story that describes the setting.

© Not to be photocopied   Section 8: Writing — Fiction Writing

Writing Stories

Writing a story might sound a tad intimidating, but they're great opportunities to get creative and let your imagination run wild. Use the previous pages in this section to help you and you'll be fine.

1. Write the opening sentence for each of the story ideas below.

   a) Two children find a time machine and accidentally travel into the future.

   b) Carys finds an old locket which allows her to see and speak to ghosts.

   c) A scientist builds a robot that malfunctions and goes on a rampage.

   d) Harriet wakes up to find that her house has moved while she was asleep.

2. Choose one of the story summaries below, then answer the questions.

   A A class suspect their teacher is an alien and set out to prove it. After uncovering the truth, they must help their teacher leave Earth and return home.

   B Eggsmeralda and Cluckbert are kidnapped on a stormy night. The rest of their brood leave the safety of the farm to embark on a daring rescue mission.

   a) What atmosphere should the story have? How will you achieve this?

   ....

   ....

   b) Think of two main characters for your story. Write a description of them which includes the following points:

• what they look like	• how they behave
• what they sound like	• their relationship with each other

   ....

   ....

   ....

   ....

   ....

   c) Plan the story, using the details from your chosen story summary to help you.

   d) Now write the full story, making sure to cover everything you included in your plan.

Section 8: Writing — Fiction Writing

Writing Scripts

With scripts, you can't rely on descriptions to show a character's thoughts. Instead, you must use clear stage directions and dialogue so that the audience knows what the character is thinking without seeing the script.

1. Write out the script below, filling in the gaps **[...]** with stage directions to show the actors what to do and how to speak.

    [LEAH tiptoes on stage with some firewood. AKIO is hidden from view behind some rocks.]

    LEAH: [...] Pssst! Akio? Are you there? I've found firewood.

    [...]

    LEAH: [...] Hey! You made me drop all the wood!

    AKIO: [...] Shhh! You're going to lead the dragon right to us!

    LEAH: Don't jump out at me then! Now help me start this fire. It's a blizzard out there.

    AKIO: [...] How is lighting a beacon for the dragon going to help Tim?

    LEAH: [...] Well I doubt freezing to death is going to help him either.

    [pauses] I'm sorry... I didn't mean to snap. I'm just scared for Tim.

    AKIO: [...] We won't let anything bad happen to him. I promise.

2. Choose one of the scenes below, then answer the questions.

    A A teacher is angry at a student who has forgotten to do their homework for the third time in a week. The student tries to give an excuse.

    B The king has been captured so his two daughters hatch a plan to rescue him. They set out on a mission where they disguise themselves as knights.

    C A teenager discovers that they are able to talk to animals. They start quizzing their dog about this strange new ability.

    a) How do you think the characters would be feeling in this scene?

    b) How do you think the characters would speak and behave?

    c) Write the scene, making sure to include the following points.

i)	stage directions that show the characters' actions
ii)	stage directions that show how the characters speak
iii)	plenty of dialogue between the characters

NOW TRY THIS: Turning something familiar into a script is a great way to practise writing one. For example, watch an episode of your favourite TV show and then have a go at writing at least a page of script for the opening scene. Think about how to introduce the setting and characters as well as the dialogue.

Poetry

There are lots of different types of poem, each with their own conventions. Some have a strict structure, like limericks. Others, like free verse, are well... more free so you don't have to follow as many rules.

1. **The poem below is about summer.**

   > The hum of a honeybee gathering pollen.
   > The heat of the sun in sapphire skies.
   > The aroma of seaweed, sun cream and brine.
   > The sweetness of ice cream in crisp wafer cones.
   > The hues of the sky turning orange at sunset.

   Remember that not all poems have to rhyme.

   a) What type of poem is this? Explain how you can tell.

   ....

   ....

   b) The poem above uses the five senses to describe summer. How would you describe winter using the senses? Give one example for each sense.

   c) Write a second stanza for the poem using your answer to part b).
   The poem doesn't have to rhyme.

2. **Write a poem about one of the topics below.**
   Choose your favourite, then answer the questions.

   | a sunset over the ocean | travelling down a river in a canoe |
   | a rainy morning in a forest | looking at cakes in a shop window |

   a) What tone do you want your poem to have? What can you do to achieve this?

   b) How do you want the reader to feel when they read your poem?

   c) Write the full poem, using this checklist to help you.

   ☐ The structure of the poem is sensible.
   ☐ The tone of the poem is appropriate for the topic.
   ☐ The poem includes some language techniques.
   ☐ The spelling, punctuation and grammar are correct.
   ☐ Interesting vocabulary has been used.

   > Paddling along in our canoe
   > Smiling, we watch the lovely view.
   > The river is a beautiful blue...
   > Crash! We almost capsized — phew!

Section 8: Writing — Fiction Writing

Section 9: Writing — Writing Properly

Whether you're writing your third best-selling fantasy novel or a first-class essay about Shakespeare, you need to make sure that your spelling, punctuation and paragraphs are correct. Lucky for you, this section goes through all the stuff you need to watch out for. Have a go at these warm-up questions first.

Before you Start

1. Which of the following are valid reasons to start a new paragraph? Tick all that apply.

   a) You're describing a new time. ☐
   b) You've used a linking phrase. ☐
   c) You're describing a new place. ☐
   d) A different person speaks. ☐
   e) You think the text will look nicer. ☐
   f) You're introducing a new topic. ☐
   g) You've written over six sentences. ☐
   h) You're giving a new point of view. ☐

2. This extract below is from a diary entry.

   > Its my birthday tomorrow and I'm finally going to be thirteen year's old. My birthday is at the start of August so all of my friend's birthdays are before mine. At least I dont have to go to school on my birthday though. When the weathers nice, we usually host a family barbecue at my grandmas' house because her garden is huge. She also makes the best birthday cake's, but it's a secret recipe.

   a) Underline the words that have used apostrophes incorrectly in the text.

   b) Rewrite the underlined words correctly.

   ....

   ....

3. Rewrite the sentences below to correct the spelling mistakes.

   a) I beleive I should practice the guitar more often.

   ....

   b) The book's main caracter is really fasinating.

   ....

   c) My doctor refered me to the hospital for treetment.

   ....

Punctuation Mix

A sprinkle of semicolons, a pinch of parentheses and a dash of... well you get the picture. Before you use all of these lovely punctuation marks in your writing, you need to make sure you understand how they work.

1. Add a colon to each of the sentences below.

    a) You need to buy these things at the shop onions, milk and cheese.

    b) We can't go camping until tomorrow it's supposed to rain today.

    c) Elijah and Beatrice were late for school they couldn't find their shoes.

    d) I'm so nervous I have a dance recital in the morning.

2. Rewrite the sentences below using brackets to separate the extra information.

    a) Wilfred Owen an English poet fought in the First World War.

    ....

    b) My cousin is getting married in the summer 21st August.

    ....

    c) The National Equine Institute for Giant Horses NEIGH is closed.

    ....

3. Each sentence below has one too many semicolons. Cross out the incorrect semicolons.

    a) Delilah played golf at the weekend; Ikenna went to a restaurant; with his friends.

    b) I wake up early; to go for a run; my sister stays in bed until eleven o'clock.

    c) Audrey has had a productive day: she finished the book; that she only started yesterday; baked a cake (a lemon one) for dessert; and tidied all of the mess on her bedroom floor.

4. Rewrite the story below so that it uses direct speech.
   Make sure that you punctuate the direct speech correctly.

   > Martha asked her mother if she had seen her skateboard. She told Martha that she should check under her bed as that was where she last saw it. Martha looked under her bed but she told her mum she still couldn't find it. Suddenly, she heard a loud noise outside and saw that her younger sister had taken her skateboard without asking. Martha bellowed at her sister to get off her skateboard before she broke it.

Structuring Your Writing

You could write the best essay in the world, but if it's just one big chunk of text then it's going to be tricky to read. You need to structure your writing with paragraphs and add linking words so that they flow together.

1. Identify where the new paragraph should start in each box below by marking it with paragraph markers (//). Then write why the new paragraph is needed on the dotted lines.

   A) Hail assailed the windows while Clara listened intently to her uncle's spooky story. She clutched her cushion for comfort. "Those who drift too close to the haunted cliffs never return…" he whispered, as if he feared the cliffs themselves might hear him.

   B) Before we begin, I want to thank you all for attending this gala. The money you have raised will greatly support the animals in our shelter. I founded this charity ten years ago with one goal: to help as many animals as I could.

   C) In the future, I would love to visit Machu Picchu. The history of the Inca Empire has always fascinated me and the photos look spectacular. To get there, you can take a train or hike from the city of Cuzco. I also want to visit Italy because I love pizza.

   ....

   ....

2. Complete the paragraphs below by correctly placing the linking words from the box.

   | Alternatively   Additionally   On the one hand |

   The personification of the forest shows that the author believes that the forest is sentient, highlighting their deep connection with the place in which they grew up.

   .... , the use of onomatopoeia lets the reader form their own connection to the forest as they can easily imagine its sounds, as if they were there too.

   .... , both of these techniques could have been used to simply help the reader better understand the importance of the forest to the author.

   .... , the author may have built this connection so that the forest's destruction is more tragic to the reader, allowing them to better understand the author's pain.

3. The plan below is for an essay about the usefulness of paper rounds. Write the essay, making sure to use linking words so that your writing flows smoothly.

   Introduction — Describe what a paper round entails.
   Point 1 — Paper rounds teach you lots of useful skills for your future career.
   Point 2 — They help you learn the value of money and how to save money.
   Point 3 — They teach you how to manage your time wisely and be responsible.
   Conclusion — A paper round is a fantastic way for teenagers to earn money.

   Write one paragraph per point.

Redrafting and Proofreading

It's perfectly normal not to get everything right the first time around. That's why you redraft and proofread your work — it helps you to find any places that need a rethink, as well as spotting any pesky mistakes.

1. The text below is a news report about a robbery.

   ☐ → Yesterday evening, an armed gang broke into G. Arnet & Sons, a local jewellers. It is estimated that the thieves stole £1.6 million worth of jewellery, mostly diamonds and watches.

   ☐ → According to CCTV footage, the thieves left the scene at precisely 8pm. They hurried from the scene to a nearby alleyway and emerged in a black van moments later. It is presumed that this van is also stolen.

   ☐ → The police want witnesses to visit them. Witnesses will need to make a statement. They need to identify the robbers. They are also looking for the owner of the stolen van.

   a) Tick the paragraph that needs to be redrafted.

   b) Explain why you think this paragraph should be redrafted.

   ....

   ....

   c) Redraft the paragraph so that it solves any problems you've mentioned in part b).

2. The extract below is from a short story. Proofread it carefully, then circle each spelling or punctuation mistake and write the correction above it.

   My energy reserves where fading as day became night. Luckily, the lighthouse iluminated the path, it's pulsing light guiding me through the shadows until Id almost reached home. Suddenly, a loud bang startled me, and I was plundged into darkness. The opressive shadows swallowed my feet and I couldn't see the next step. I took a deep breath: may be everything would be fine if I could make it too the bridge near my house. I stumbled to where the old whethered posts ought to be and gingerly felt for the first plank. However I found something scarier; absolutely nothing

> **NOW TRY THIS** — Write a short speech about something you want to change in the world. Read what you've written and identify any points that need improving, then redraft your speech. Proofread your final draft, paying close attention to any mistakes with grammar, punctuation or spelling.

Section 10: Writing — Making It Interesting

Now you've practised your punctuation and paragraphs, it's time to look at how you can make your writing interesting and engaging as well as correct. You can do this by adding figurative language or exciting adjectives into your writing, or just by adding a little bit of variety to your sentences.

Before you Start

1. Replace the underlined words in the sentences below to make them more interesting.

   a) The weather was <u>nice</u> so I <u>walked</u> through the park.

   ....

   b) Robin <u>checked</u> the <u>weird</u> noise in the attic.

   ....

2. Write down the figurative language technique from the box that each sentence is using.

   a) Frosty leaves crunched under my boots.   ....

   b) The waterfall was a roaring lion.   ....

   c) Teresa's face was as red as a ripe tomato.   ....

   d) Jamil can swim faster than a speedboat.   ....

   e) The stars wink at me from the dark sky.   ....

personification
onomatopoeia
simile
exaggeration (hyperbole)
metaphor

3. a) Draw lines to match each text to the improvement it needs (**i-iii**).

   A I got to the cinema then I bought some popcorn then I sat down then I waited for the film to start.

   B Manuel was most aggrieved by the tardiness with which his luncheon had materialised.

   C It was mean of those children to play a mean prank on Beth. She wasn't even mean to them.

   i) Make some of the complex words more simple.

   ii) Replace the repeated adjectives.

   iii) Turn the long sentence into two short ones.

   b) Rewrite each sentence, making the improvement you picked in part a).

Using Different Techniques

There are lots of ways to make your writing more interesting. You could vary the length of your sentences, shake up your vocabulary or describe things using comparisons. The world's your oyster, really.

1. The sentences below have used comparisons to make their descriptions more interesting.

   a) Tick the sentences that have used comparisons correctly.

   i) Jacqueline is the least enthusiastic player on the team. ☐

   ii) The sea was as blue as a sapphire and just as beautiful. ☐

   iii) Last summer was hotter than a stale loaf of bread. ☐

   iv) Alice was more happier than a mouse in a cheese factory. ☐

   b) Rewrite the incorrect sentences so that they use comparisons correctly.

   ....

   ....

2. Read the texts below, then answer the questions.

   A Snow was falling heavily, so I couldn't see how far it was to the road where Disha lives with her nan, who is a really good baker. The cold reminded me of when I went skiing in Norway at Christmas when I was little.

   B Thunder rumbled outside. It was loud. I'm scared of thunder. I ran upstairs. My bed felt safe. Another rumble. It was closer this time. I hid under the covers. There was a flash. Then another rumble. I wanted it to end.

   a) Briefly explain how each text could be made more interesting.

   ....

   ....

   ....

   b) Pick one of the passages above and rewrite it to make it more interesting.

3. Rewrite the passage below so each sentence starts differently.

   He went to the zoo last weekend. He bought a map and some feed for the goats in the petting zoo. He really liked the apes, especially the baby gorilla. He thought the snakes were quite scary though. He bought a burger for lunch. He also bought a magnet for his fridge as a souvenir.

   You could link some sentences together to make your passage more interesting too.

Section 10: Writing — Making It Interesting

Figurative Language

Adding figurative language to your writing is a great way to engage the reader. There are five main types that you should get to grips with: similes, metaphors, hyperbole, personification and onomatopoeia.

1. Rewrite the sentences below so that each sentence uses a metaphor to create the same meaning.

   a) The crowd laughed hysterically.

   ....

   b) Farah has green eyes.

   ....

   c) The fridge was empty.

   ....

2. Have a think about your journey to school. Write three similes to describe what you see along the way.

   ....

   ....

   ....

   ....

3. The passage below could be improved with some figurative language.

   > <u>The old train was noisily making its way through the landscape.</u> We seemed to be leaving all traces of civilisation behind. Even the old, dilapidated farmhouses were becoming less and less frequent. <u>I was very nervous.</u> It was the first time I'd ever left the city. I pulled my book out of my bag and began to read. It was a book I'd had since I was five years old. <u>Its pages were familiar and comforting.</u>

   Rewrite the underlined sentences to include one of the following figurative language techniques. You should only use each technique once.

   a) personification   b) onomatopoeia   c) exaggeration (hyperbole)

NOW TRY THIS — It's time to use everything you've learnt in this section. Continue the story in Question 3 by writing a couple of paragraphs about where the narrator ends up. Try to include a few types of figurative language and check your writing for any adjectives or verbs that could be made more interesting.

Section 11: Writing Review

Now that you've finished going through the writing section of the book, it's time to put everything you've learnt into practice. The questions over the next two pages will help you to write a story.

> Your local council is running a campaign to encourage more teenagers to explore and protect nature. As part of this campaign, they are publishing a book filled with adventure stories set in the natural world that are written by teenagers from your school.
>
> Write an adventure story set in the great outdoors. Your story should include:
> - a description of the setting where the adventure takes place
> - something that puts the setting in danger
> - a strategy to save the setting of the story

1. a) What is the purpose of the story?

to argue ☐   to entertain ☐   to inform ☐   to explain ☐

☐ 1 mark

b) What do you think you need to do to achieve this purpose?

....

....

☐ 1 mark

2. a) Who is going to read your story?

....

☐ 1 mark

b) How are you going to make your story suitable for the audience?

....

....

☐ 1 mark

3. a) Choose a setting that would be suitable for your story. Explain your choice.

....

....

☐ 2 marks

b) Write three sentences that describe the setting you have chosen.

☐ 3 marks

Writing Review

4. a) Write down three character traits for your main character.

....

1 mark

b) How could you use your character's actions to reflect the character traits you wrote down in part a)? Give one idea for each trait.

These answers don't have to be in your final story. They're here to get you thinking about your character.

3 marks

c) Give two ways that your character's appearance could reflect their personality.

....

....

2 marks

5. Use the table below to plan the structure of your story. Refer back to the instructions on p.78 to make sure you're including everything you have been asked to write about.

Engaging opening	
Plot development 1	
Plot development 2	
Plot development 3	
Satisfying ending	

5 marks

6. How could you use the structure of your story to create suspense? Give two ways.

....

....

2 marks

7. Now write your story in full. Aim to write about two paragraphs for each plot development. Use your answers to the previous questions and the plan you made in Question 5 to help you.

10 marks

When you've finished writing your story, make sure you read through it to check for any mistakes.

Writing Review

Practise fiction skills — check. Now let's see how much you can remember about non-fiction texts. The questions on this page will help you plan an answer to an argument text for the scenario below.

> Your school has decided to stop teaching all language classes. This is an extract from the official report written by your headteacher.
>
> As of next year, French, Spanish and German classes will no longer be part of our curriculum. Instead, we will offer additional classes in English, maths and science. We believe these subjects are more important to our students' post-16 careers. By offering more time to practise these three subjects, our students should receive better grades. This will improve the status and reputation of our school in the local community.
>
> Write a letter to the headteacher of your school, arguing that languages should still be taught in your school.

1. What do you think the tone of your argument should be? Explain why.

   ....

   ....

   2 marks

2. Think of three arguments against what your headteacher has said in their report. Then, use these to help you plan your letter. Make sure you include an engaging introduction and a convincing conclusion.

   6 marks

3. Choose one of your arguments from Question 2. Plan your chosen argument in more detail.

   2 marks

4. Choose one of the arguments you wrote down for Question 2, then use it to construct a detailed counter argument against one of your headteacher's points.

   ....

   ....

   ....

   2 marks

5. Now write your letter in full. Aim to write a paragraph for each argument. Use your answers to the questions above to help you. Don't forget to reread your finished letter and correct any mistakes.

   10 marks

Section 11: Writing Review © Not to be photocopied

Writing Review

You've made it to the last page of questions. *sobs* I'm so proud. I've said it before and I'll say it again — plan your answer before you start writing and check for any mistakes when you've finished.

Professor Gold E. Lochs is visiting your town to judge the Annual Literary Festival. The main event includes a fairy tale competition. This year's theme is good vs. evil.

Your fairy tale should include:

- a description of the setting
- detailed descriptions of a hero and a villain that show their personalities
- a conflict between the two characters

Write your fairy tale for the competition.

10 marks

Your local supermarket is trying to encourage its customers to live a healthier lifestyle. They want you to write an advice leaflet to give to customers as they enter the shop.

This is what they would like you to include:

- an explanation of the importance of exercising and eating a balanced diet
- suggestions for healthier alternatives to unhealthy foods
- suggestions for ways to integrate exercise easily into their daily routine

Write your advice leaflet for the supermarket.

10 marks

Your local drama club has asked you to write a short script to explore what life would be like for teenagers if all social media suddenly stopped working.

You should include:

- how different teenagers feel about what has happened
- helpful stage directions for the actors
- an appropriate resolution to the story — does social media start working again or not?

Write your script for the drama club.

10 marks

Your school wants suggestions of places that would make enjoyable, educational trips for students next year. Write an essay about one place that you would suggest, explaining why it is a suitable choice for a school trip.

You should include:

- a brief description of the place you are suggesting
- reasons why you think it is suitable
- evidence to support the reasons you have given

Write your essay about a possible school trip destination.

10 marks

Answers

Section 1: Reading — Audience and Purpose

Page 3 — Before you Start

1. **a)** Fable — A short story which has a moral
Myth — A made-up story about gods or heroes
Play — A story which is performed and has stage directions
   b) You should have ticked: to entertain
2. You should have circled:
pet owners
a beginner
3.

Text	Audience	Purpose
A	young children	to inform
B	parents	to advise
C	schoolchildren	to persuade

Page 4 — Different Types of Texts

1. **a)** Any sensible answer, e.g.
   i) A — a science textbook
   ii) B — instructions
   b) Any sensible explanation, e.g. Extract A explains clearly how a scientific process takes place, which suggests it is from a textbook. Extract B instructs the reader on how to apply paint effectively, which suggests it is from a set of instructions.
2. **a)** A speech
   b) Any sensible answer, e.g. The text addresses the audience directly, using pronouns and rhetorical questions.
   c) i) Opinion
   ii) Fact
   iii) Opinion
   d) Any fact from the text, e.g.
   Less than a tenth of authors and illustrators are from a minority ethnic background.

Page 5 — Audience

1. **a)** expert historians
   b) friends
   c) newspaper readers
2. **a)** You should have circled: B
   b) Any sensible answer, e.g. Text B is most suitable for adults with no baking experience as it uses simple language and step-by-step instructions.
   c) Any sensible answer, e.g. Adults with baking experience, because it uses technical terms like "sift" which only people with baking experience would know.
   d) Any sensible answer where Text B is rewritten to use simple vocabulary and instructions so it is suitable for young children. E.g.
   1. Melt the chocolate and butter in a bowl.
   2. Break the eggs into the bowl and mix everything together with a spoon.
   3. Place a sieve on top of the bowl and pour the flour through the sieve. Ask your parents for help with this step.
   4. Stir the mixture carefully until there are no lumpy bits.

Page 6 — Purpose

1. **a)** to entertain — B
to argue — C
to inform — D
to advise — A
   b) Any sensible answer, e.g.
   Extract A gives a suggestion to advise the reader.
   Extract B uses lots of imagery to entertain the reader.
   Extract C uses exaggerated language to argue a point.
   Extract D uses a fact to inform the reader.
2. **a)** You should have ticked: to complain
   b) Any sensible answer, e.g. The writer explains to the owner of the café that they were unhappy with the experience they had there. They use strong adjectives like "abominable" and "repulsive" to show how unsatisfied they were.
3. **a)** Any sensible answer, e.g. The facts about the books could be used to give polite suggestions to advise someone about what to read.
   b) Any sensible answer that uses the information in the text and gives polite suggestions that advise someone about what to read, e.g.
   If you enjoy reading fantasy books, I would recommend *Escape to Albion*. It's a novel about King Arthur, set in the modern age. It's got a great combination of comedy, drama and romance, so it should keep you entertained. Alternatively, if you don't have time to read a whole novel, you could try *Kiki and the Castle*, which is a short story about a girl who discovers an ancient castle.

Page 7 — Context

1. **a) i)** Any sensible answer, e.g. Mr Trabb speaks to Pip very politely and respectfully, calling him "sir".
   ii) Any sensible answer, e.g. It suggests that wealth was highly valued and admired, because Mr Trabb immediately shows respect to Pip once he realises he is rich.

2 a) E.g. "War has its horrors"
  b) Any sensible answer, e.g. He thinks that war sorts the good, brave men from the cowards.
  c) Any sensible answer, e.g. The extract suggests that the narrator thinks soldiers should be honoured as "brave" and "intrepid". The image of soldiers as "the cream" which has been skimmed off mankind suggests that soldiers are the best of humanity, far better than the "world of cowards" that they are fighting to protect.

Section 2: Reading — Non-Fiction Texts

Page 8 — Before you Start

1 a) Any sensible answer, e.g. To inform the reader about the event. It gives the reader a number of details, for example that the shark was spotted "just offshore from a popular beach" and stayed there "for several hours".
  b) Any sensible answer, e.g. She agrees with the coastguard. The text says that she "welcomes" the coastguard's advice. She also adds additional information to support the coastguard's advice.
  c) i) Any sensible answer, e.g. It makes me feel a little concerned but then also reassured.
  ii) Any sensible explanation, e.g. It concerns me because I didn't realise there were sharks in the UK, but I feel reassured because the article says that the shark poses "very little threat".
  d) Any sensible summary of the article using your own words, e.g.
  Holidaymakers spotted a shark near to a popular beach. The shark was unlikely to be a risk to the public, but both the coastguard and a local marine wildlife charity asked people to keep their distance.

Page 9 — Finding Evidence in the Text

1 a)

How long did it take to prepare for the Moon landing?	eight years
Where did the astronauts begin their journey?	The Kennedy Space Center in Florida
How many more times has NASA sent people to the Moon?	five
When is NASA planning to send more astronauts to the Moon?	by 2024

  b) Any sensible answer, e.g. There is a "tense wait" for the Eagle to land "safely". This suggests that the descent could have gone dangerously wrong.
  c) Millions of people watched it live on television.
  d) "it remains a pivotal moment in human history"

Page 10 — Summarising

1 a) i) You should have ticked: disappointed
  ii) You should have ticked: gripped
  b) Any sensible answer, e.g.
  Author A was disappointed because they had high expectations for the film but they thought that the actors did not perform to the best of their abilities. They also found the plot unimaginative and the characters unoriginal. Author B was gripped because of the film's action and the exciting unpredictability of the plot.

2 a) i) Any sensible answer, e.g. angry and frustrated
  ii) Any sensible summary, e.g. The author is angry because they think that the public transport in their country is very bad. They criticise the unreliability of trains and buses, and are frustrated by the price of trains. They think that these issues make people use cars instead, which causes pollution and congestion.
  b) i) Any sensible title, e.g. 'Public Transport: Over-priced, Unreliable and Unacceptable'
  ii) Any sensible explanation, e.g. I chose this title because it summarises the main complaints about public transport that the author makes in their speech.

Page 11 — Working Out What's Going On

1 a) They got their name from their large size.
  b) They were much larger than the dinosaurs that had already been discovered, and they are currently the largest land animals known to have existed.
  c) No — the leaflet says that their predictions are based on "incomplete evidence", so the predictions may need to change if more evidence comes to light.
  d) i) Any sensible answer, e.g. The author is impressed.
  ii) Any sensible explanation, e.g. The author describes the discovery as an "astonishing achievement", which suggests they are very impressed.
  e) Any sensible answer, e.g. Yes, there could be some even larger dinosaurs. Until the titanosaurs were discovered, people thought that sauropods were the largest dinosaurs, but this proved not to be the case. The extract suggests that our understanding may change again, and that "new discoveries" may be made.

Page 12 — Layout and Structure

1 a) You should have ticked:
to summarise what the park has to offer

b) Any sensible answer, e.g.
To draw attention to the low cost of the holiday ("FREE" and "AFFORDABLE"), and the need to book quickly ("NOW"). This helps to convince the reader that the holiday is worth booking without delay.

c) Any sensible answer that picks out two features of the first lines and mentions their effect on the reader, e.g.
Yes, the introduction is effective. The use of a rhetorical question engages the reader and gets them to think about their holiday plans. Writing "AFFORDABLE" in upper-case letters makes Elmsmere Holiday Park more appealing to the reader, as it makes it seem like it's good value for money.

d) Any sensible answer, e.g.
To convince the reader to book the holiday right away. Emphasising the words, "NOW" and "LIMITED-TIME OFFER" using upper-case letters encourages them to act quickly in case they miss the offer.

2 Any sensible answer that explains why the layout isn't appropriate for a recipe and suggests how it could be improved, e.g.
Having one large chunk of text makes it difficult for the reader to follow the steps in the recipe. There is also no list of equipment or ingredients, so it isn't immediately clear what is needed for the recipe. The text could be split into three separate parts (equipment, ingredients and method) so the reader can see what they need before they start. The instructions for the method could be split into numbered parts so the steps are easier to follow.

Pages 13-14 — Language Techniques

1 a) presented with such a prestigious prize — alliteration
progress was a million times slower than you could possibly imagine — exaggeration
life is a road paved with opportunities — metaphor

b) Any sensible explanation, e.g.
The author uses these techniques in their speech to engage their listeners. They help the author to vividly express the effort they put into their work and their excitement at winning the prize.

2 a) Any two examples of descriptive language, e.g. "the valley may still be concealing some of its deepest secrets from them", "the guards are like hawks"

b) Any sensible explanation, e.g.
Travel guides are often read by people who are looking for good places to travel. Using descriptive language makes the Valley of the Kings seem more vivid and interesting, so it seems like an attractive place to visit.

3 a) i) A — 'list of three', "deep, earthy, warming tones"
B — rhetorical questions, e.g. "Tired of tuna mayo?"

ii) Any sensible answer, e.g. The list of three adjectives in Extract A helps the reader to vividly imagine the scent of the candle. The rhetorical questions in Extract B grab the reader's attention by directly addressing them.

iii) Any sensible answer, e.g. Extract A is a review which advises the reader to buy a candle, and Extract B is an advert for a product. Therefore both extracts use persuasive writing to persuade the reader to buy something.

b) i) E.g. "thrilling discovery"

ii) Any sensible answer, e.g. It makes the reader excited about the discovery and makes them want to learn more about how it could change their life.

Page 15 — Tone

1 a) i) You should have ticked: overwhelmed

ii) Any sensible explanation, e.g.
The writer says they have "a lot to be getting on with", which suggests they are very busy. They also seem stressed by the amount of unpacking they have do in "there's just so much stuff and nowhere to put it!"

b) i) Any sensible answer, e.g. formal / serious
ii) Any sensible answer, e.g. helpful / friendly
iii) Any sensible answer, e.g. informal / chatty

2 a) Text A's tone is very formal and impersonal. Text B is friendly and informal in tone.

b) Any sensible answer, e.g. I don't think that the tone of Text A is appropriate for its purpose. It is supposed to be a note to a close friend, but it sounds too formal. However, I think the friendly tone of Text B is appropriate for its purpose as it will encourage people to attend the reopening of the pub.

Page 16 — What You Think

1 a) Any sensible answer, e.g. It makes the reader feel as if they are involved and should be on the author's side.

b) i) Any sensible adjectives, e.g. formal and critical
ii) Any sensible answer, e.g.
The formal tone makes the reader take the text seriously. The critical tone encourages the reader to agree with the author and think that people in favour of school uniforms are wrong.

c) Any sensible opinion that is supported with an explanation, e.g.
I think school uniform should be abolished. Although some feel that having a uniform makes students equal, families can end up spending an extortionate amount of money on clothes that pupils will grow out of very quickly.

d) Any sensible answer, e.g.
The author does not present a balanced view of the topic as the focus of the text is weighted against school uniform. There are three arguments against school uniform and two arguments for it. The arguments in favour of school uniform have come from just one student who is written about in the third person. This distances their opinion from the opinion expressed in the first person.

Page 17 — The Author's Intentions

1 a) i) interesting — the castle (C)
disappointing — the memorial garden (B)
unsettling — the statues (D)
surprising — the cathedral (A)

ii) Any sensible explanations, e.g.
The author describes an exhibit about the castle's history as "fascinating", which suggests it was interesting.
The author suggests that the memorial garden was not as nice as they expected it to be by highlighting how noisy, busy and untidy it was. This makes it seem disappointing.
The author calls the statues "intimidating", and describes standing under them as an "unpleasant feeling", which makes them seem unsettling.
The author creates a contrast between the "drab" outside of the cathedral and its inside, which was "completely different" and full of colour and detail. This highlights that the cathedral was surprisingly good.

b) i) The author presents the castle (Extract C) most positively.

ii) Any sensible explanation, e.g. The author uses strongly positive language and a positive tone, describing the exhibit about the castle's history as "fascinating" and the view from the ramparts as "spectacular". This gives the reader the impression that they would enjoy visiting the castle. In contrast, the author refers to the drawbacks of the other attractions, which makes them seem less attractive than the castle.

Section 3: Reading — Fiction and Plays

Page 18 — Before you Start

1 a) Any sensible summary, e.g. Anna feels exhilarated and focused as she gets ready to start the race.

b) Any sensible answer, e.g. As soon as the starting pistol has been fired.

c) Any sensible answer, e.g. To highlight Anna's new sense of determination. The short, simple sentences reflect Anna's single-mindedness as she vows to escape from Agent One.

d) i) You should have ticked: afraid but determined

ii) Any sensible explanation, e.g. Anna trembles at the sight of Agent One, suggesting she is afraid. However, she seems determined when she vows that she "couldn't — wouldn't" let herself be caught.

e) Any sensible answer, e.g.
The mood is exciting and tense as Anna prepares to take part in the race. After Anna sees Agent One, the mood becomes uneasy and threatening as Anna's fear of Agent One becomes obvious.

Page 19 — Finding Evidence in the Text

1 a) i) Frank Churchill has proposed to Miss Fairfax.

ii) You should have circled: He had already heard it from someone else.

b)

How Emma feels about ignoring Mr Knightley's warning	"with a sinking voice and a heavy sigh" OR "I wish I had attended to it"
Mr Knightley's view of Frank Churchill	"Abominable scoundrel!"
Mr Knightley's view of Miss Fairfax	"I am sorry for her. She deserves a better fate."

c) Any sensible answer which is backed up by details from the text, e.g.
He holds her arm and presses it "against his heart". He then consoles her with comforting words, telling her that "time will heal the wound". He also states that he has "feelings of the warmest friendship" towards her, and is angry on her behalf.

Page 20 — Summarising

1 a) Any sensible summary, e.g.
Gemma feels sorry for herself because she has been abandoned by Jodie.

b) Any sensible summary, e.g.
Gemma and Jodie were best friends and used to be virtually inseparable.

c) Any sensible summary, e.g.
They grew apart because they have different interests. Jodie enjoys sports and increasingly spent time with her team mates rather than Gemma.

d) i) You should have ticked:
Gemma feels upset because she has grown apart from her best friend.

ii) Any sensible explanation, e.g.
The extract mainly focuses on how Gemma feels and how her relationship with her best friend, Jodie, has broken down. Therefore this is the best summary because it focuses both on Gemma being "upset" and how she has "grown apart" from Jodie. The first sentence doesn't mention how Gemma feels, and the third sentence doesn't cover any of these key ideas.

Page 21 — Working Out What's Going On

1. a) You should have ticked:
   i) True
   ii) True
   iii) False
   b) "Sunshine prickles deliciously against the skin of my face."
   c) Any sensible answer, e.g. It suggests that there isn't much wildlife in London anymore because the narrator no longer sees a common insect like a ladybird.
   d) Any sensible answer, e.g. The author uses a metaphor to show the narrator feels trapped in London. The narrator calls London a "prison-city" and finds comfort in imagining that their evaporating sweat is "staging an invisible escape". This suggests that the narrator is unable to leave London and relishes any sense of freedom they can find.

Page 22 — Structure

1. a) You should have circled:
   There is a flashback in the narrative.
   b) Any sensible answer, e.g.
   They help to order Talia's complicated narrative so it is easier to follow.
   c) Any sensible answer, e.g.
   It emphasises Talia's defensiveness, as it suggests that she knew what she was doing until Sam did something completely unpredictable.
   d) Any sensible answer, e.g.
   The crossed-out bits of text show what the narrator is really thinking even though she wouldn't admit it out loud.
   e) Any sensible answer, e.g
   It makes Talia seem stressed and jumbled because she launches straight into defending herself over the situation with Sam before even introducing herself.
   f) Any sensible answer, e.g. I think it is effective because it poses a problem to the reader that Talia will later have to solve, so the reader is keen to know how she does this.

Page 23 — Themes

1. a) Any sensible answer, e.g.
   The extract describes a crime: the Dodger and Charley Bates steal a handkerchief from an elderly gentleman.
   b) You should have ticked:
   i) True
   ii) False
   iii) False
   c) Any sensible answer, e.g.
   They select their victim expertly and commit the crime smoothly and confidently, sneaking up behind the gentleman, stealing his handkerchief and running away.
   d) i) Any sensible answer, e.g.
   Oliver appears shocked and horrified by crime. He watches the theft with "horror and alarm" and then runs away, "tingling" with "terror".
   ii) Any sensible answer, e.g.
   The other boys have a completely different attitude to crime to Oliver. They view crime as acceptable and it seems to be part of their daily lives. While Oliver panics when he witnesses the crime, they seem to be calm and in control when carrying out the theft.

Page 24 — Language Techniques

1. a) i) The fields were like crinkled-up grey blankets — simile
   the bleating crickets and cracking thin limbs of the trees — onomatopoeia
   the house letting out a muffled sneery snort — personification
   ii) Any sensible answer, e.g.
   The onomatopoeia of "bleating" and "cracking" helps the reader imagine the sounds that the narrator hears.
   The simile comparing the fields to "crinkled-up grey blankets" vividly describes how the uneven furrows of the fields look during the night.
   The personification makes the house seem alive, and suggests that the narrator feels mocked by everyone and everything, including things that aren't alive.
   b) You should have underlined:
   "like a bony fingermark on a black cloth"
   "the moon was fading, getting thin like tissue"
   Any sensible explanation, e.g.
   The descriptions "bony" and "black" create an ominous, spooky atmosphere. The comparison between the moon and tissue vividly emphasises how thin and fragile the moon appears.
   c) Any sensible answer, e.g.
   The author uses personification to make it seem as if the house is alive. For example, the house behaves like a human: it looks at the narrator, snorts and pretends to be something it is not.
   d) Any sensible answer, e.g.
   The house is described as an outsider because it is a different colour to the other houses and it perches "awkwardly" on the hill. This reflects the narrator's own feelings of not fitting in. However, the house is also personified so that it seems to be judging the narrator, watching her "smugly" and seeming to snort in the "sneery", judgemental manner her mother did. In this way, the house reinforces the narrator's feeling of exclusion, as even the strange green house that "doesn't look right" seems to reject her.

Pages 25-26 — Understanding the Characters

1. a) True
   b) True
   c) False
2. a) i) To make his life return to normal.
      ii) Any sensible answer, e.g. This suggests that Zak is unhappy and is desperate to change his situation.
   b) Any sensible answer, e.g.
      Zak has a close relationship with his dad. For example, he remembers lots of happy times he spent with his dad, walking "hand in hand".
   c) Any sensible answer, e.g.
      The author uses a simile about a leaf to show that Zak feels out of control. Zak says he feels "like a leaf" whose direction is affected by others, with no control over where he will end up. Therefore, his inability to catch the leaf symbolises that he is unable to take control of his own life.
3. a) i) You should have ticked: impatient and daring
      ii) Any sensible explanation, e.g. Billy seems impatient because he wants the book "today" and doesn't want to wait for his mother to sign the form. He seems daring because he steals the book right in front of the librarian.
   b) Any sensible answer, e.g. It suggests Billy is cheeky and bold, because he still behaves politely and draws attention to himself after having stolen the book.
   c) Any sensible answer, e.g. The librarian seems firm but fair. She is firm when she refuses to let Billy have the book because it would be "against the rules", even though Billy asks her for the book many times. However, she treats Billy fairly, telling him he can have the book if he gets his form signed.

Pages 27-28 — Understanding the Setting

1. a) You should have circled: Jamaica
   b) "A hot Jamaican sun was setting"
   c) Any two sensible examples of sensory language, e.g. The island is described as having a "balmy aroma". There is also a "cooling breeze" on the island.
   d) Any sensible answer, e.g.
      The adjective "ramshackle" suggests that the houses were hurriedly constructed, while the description of the "patchwork" of roofs makes the dwellings seem charming.
   e) Any sensible answer, e.g.
      The north side of the island is run-down, but it is described positively through imagery such as a "cooling breeze". In contrast, the south side of the island is described as inhospitable and threatening.
   f) Any sensible answer, e.g.
      The author describes the sun as a "yellow eye" which is said to "rage" over the flat Southern plains. This personification suggests that the sun is a threatening and angry force, which makes the southern part of the island seem dangerous and inhospitable. The author also describes how crocodiles "swam silently in swampy rivers" on the southern side, suggesting that there are hidden dangers there.
2. a) a carpet
   b) "shade as dense as that of velvet curtains"
   c) i) You should have ticked: grand
      ii) Any sensible answer, e.g.
         The setting is described as an "extension of a luxurious interior" of the house, which suggests that the garden is just as luxurious as the house itself. There are "rich-coloured rugs" in the garden, which emphasises how grand it is.
   d) Any sensible answer, e.g.
      It suggests that the people who live there are very wealthy and private, as the house is expensive and privacy "reigned supreme".
   e) Any sensible adjective, e.g. peaceful
      Any sensible explanation, e.g. The house is surrounded by a large garden where "Privacy reigned supreme", which makes the setting seem secluded and peaceful. The "still" trees cast a shade over the garden as though it is covered by "velvet curtains". This suggests that the garden is quiet and calm.

Pages 29-30 — Interpreting Plays

1. a) You should have ticked: irritable and inflexible
   b) Any sensible answer, e.g.
      The driver gets annoyed very easily with the children and Mrs Kay, which shows that he is irritable. He is inflexible because he forces Mrs Kay to search the children to check they don't have chocolate and lemonade.
   c) Any sensible answer, e.g.
      She is making a joke because the driver is so grumpy he is the opposite of "Mr Happiness".
   d) Any sensible answer, e.g.
      It suggests that Mrs Kay is very protective over the children, as she feels furious when the driver behaves unreasonably towards them. However, it also suggests that she is good at controlling her emotions, because she doesn't act on her anger and frustration at the driver.
2. a) i) "I am a fool / To weep at what I am glad of."
      ii) "with a heart as willing / As bondage e'er of freedom."
   b) Prospero approves of their relationship.
      Any sensible explanation, e.g.
      Prospero calls the affection between the couple "fair" and asks the "Heavens" to "rain grace / On" (bless) their relationship.

c) Any sensible answer, e.g.
Ferdinand uses a list of three verbs to do with love and devotion to emphasise his love for Miranda when he promises to "love, prize, honour" her. Ferdinand also uses exaggeration to emphasise his feelings. He argues that he loves Miranda "Beyond all limit of what else i' th' world", meaning he loves her more than anything else in the whole world.

Page 31 — Staging and Performance

1 a) You should have underlined:
"Gentlemen, rise"
"Sit, worthy friends"
"Pray you, keep seat. / Feed, and regard him not."
   b) i) Any sensible answer, e.g.
Macbeth feels afraid and angry that the ghost has appeared.
     ii) The actor should stand still as if frozen in fear, and speak in a scared but angry tone.
   c) Any sensible answer, e.g.
Lady Macbeth could whisper angrily in Macbeth's ear, gesturing in frustration at the stool. This would emphasise her anger with Macbeth, but also show that she doesn't want the Lords to become suspicious of them.
   d) Any sensible answer, e.g.
The ghost of Banquo shouldn't be shown on stage because in the scene only Macbeth can see it. Not showing the ghost would make Macbeth seem insane, as it would seem to the audience that he is hallucinating.
OR
The ghost of Banquo should be shown on stage because it would make the scene more frightening and thrilling for the audience, as Macbeth's vision would seem real.

Page 32 — What You Think

1 a) Death
   b) i) You should have circled: cold but reassuring
     ii) Any sensible answer, e.g.
The narrator seems cold because he speaks bluntly about death, declaring "You are going to die." However, the narrator softens his blunt statements with kind and reassuring words such as "Please, trust me."
   c) Any sensible answer, e.g.
It makes the reader feel like the narrator is directly addressing them, which gives the text more impact.
   d) Any sensible answer, e.g.
The narrator seems polite and pleasant because they speak to the reader in a chatty and civil manner. However, their declaration that they "can" be "amiable. Agreeable. Affable.", implies that they are not always kind and caring. This suggests that they are only trying to appear pleasant and well-mannered. This makes them seem a little unsettling, as it is not clear to the reader whether their politeness is genuine.

Section 4: Reading — Poetry

Page 33 — Before you Start

1 a) Any sensible answer, e.g. the afterlife
   b) Any sensible answer, e.g. The poet is addressing somebody they love.
   c) You should have ticked: repetition
   d) The word "Remember" is repeated.
Any sensible explanation, e.g.
The repetition of the word "Remember" conveys the strength of the narrator's desire to be remembered by the reader.
   e) Any sensible answer, e.g.
The narrator wants the person they love to remember them, but they don't want them to feel guilty if they forget the narrator at times. They say that it is better to "forget and smile" for a while than remember their grief and remain sad.

Page 34 — Working Out What's Going On

1 a) You should have ticked: The poet is describing the park's reflection in the pond.
   b) i) Any sensible quote, e.g. "birds coast belly-up"
     ii) Any sensible answer, e.g.
The pond's reflection makes everything look as if it is upside down, so birds flying through the park look as if they are flying "belly-up".
   c) A swan dips its beak into the pond which causes ripples in the water.
   d) Any sensible summary, e.g.
The narrator describes the reflection of the bridge in the water, then describes what is happening on the bridge. Barking dogs and people in hats are walking over the bridge, while a baby holding a pink balloon is being held out so they can feed the ducks.

Page 35 — Structure

1 a) Any sensible answer, e.g.
The poem starts by focusing on the person the narrator allows others to see, then moves inwards to focus on the parts of the narrator that they hide from others.
   b) Any sensible answer, e.g.
Each stanza describes another side of the narrator's character, in the same way that a Russian doll contains many different dolls inside it.
   c) i) You should have circled: "quick, slick", "joker with a poking", "scurrying, worrying" and "miss whisperer"
     ii) Any sensible answer, e.g.
The internal rhymes reflect the personality traits described in each stanza. For example, in the third stanza, it draws attention to the cleverness of the "quick, slick" character.

d) i) Any sensible answer, e.g.
The final stanza has shorter lines than the rest of the poem, and the first and last line of the stanza rhyme. The start of the stanza also does not use the repeated opening line used in the other stanzas in the poem.

ii) Any sensible explanation, e.g.
The shorter lines reflect the fact that the smallest doll is being described in the stanza. The use of rhyme creates a sense of completion, which reflects how the narrator has reached the innermost version of herself. By not repeating the phrase "And inside there's another me", the narrator makes it clear that there is nothing left to reveal.

Page 36 — Themes

1 a) i) You should have ticked: happiness

ii) Any sensible answer, e.g. The narrator uses a simile to compare their happiness to the joy that "prisoned birds" must feel when they are given their "freedom".

iii) Any sensible answer, e.g. He is happy because the war is over and he is free from its "horror".

b) Any sensible answer, e.g.
The poet is suggesting that those who die during the war and cannot be found are still remembered by God, as they are "On his Repealless-List".

c) Any sensible answer, e.g.
To make the soldiers' deaths seem natural and painless. The narrator compares the soldiers' deaths to things in nature that come and go naturally, such as "Flakes" of snow and petals on flowers.

Page 37 — Voice

1 a) The speaker is someone whose ancestors have been enslaved. They are addressing other people who are descended from slaves.

b) i) Informal
Any sensible quote, e.g. "Till the worlds slaves"

ii) Any sensible answer, e.g.
It makes the poem feel more personal, which encourages the reader to feel close to the speaker and united with them in their shared cause.

c) Any sensible answer, e.g.
It shows that the narrator isn't alone in their desire for freedom. The narrator starts by focusing on their right to be their own person, but this becomes a united call for freedom when the narrator starts using the first person plural.

d) i) Any three sensible adjectives, e.g.
empowering, inclusive and confident

ii) Any sensible explanation, e.g.
The poem's tone is empowering because it calls readers to action by asking them to "raise" their "voices" until "equality is no longer a dream". The repetition of "Got the right to be" adds to this empowering tone by arguing that everyone has the right to be free and to be themselves.

Page 38 — Techniques

1 a) Any sensible example, e.g.
"The music will not sit in straight lines."
"The notes refuse to perch on wires"
Any sensible answer, e.g.
It makes the music seem alive and rebellious, because it refuses to be restrained.

b) Any sensible answer, e.g.
It creates a strong sense of movement.

c) Any sensible answer, e.g. The lack of punctuation means the poem flows smoothly with few disruptions. This mirrors the flow of music.

d) You should have underlined:
"round the face of the clock"
"the dandelion head of time"
"circle back"
"spun / past the face of the moon"
"The cycle begins"
Any sensible answer, e.g. The repetition of circles emphasises the constant, never-ending movement of music. This adds to the smooth and flowing feel of the poem.

Section 5: Reading — Comparing Texts

Page 39 — Before you Start

1 a) i) simile

ii) "as sorry as a cat in a bath"
"shaking like a leaf"

b) i) Any sensible answer, e.g. The tone is angry at first as the author vows that Victor will be "sorry". The tone shifts to pleased when the narrator discusses their "inventive prank", then it becomes sheepish when things get "out of hand".

ii) Any sensible answer, e.g. Text B has a more serious and detached tone than Text A because it is a newspaper article. It reports the facts of the lion sighting using formal language and without offering any opinions on the events being reported.

c) Any two differences, e.g.
The texts have a different layout. Text A uses subheadings to show what day the writer is writing in their diary. Text B uses a headline and columns because it is a newspaper article. Language techniques are used in Text B to engage the reader. For example, the alliteration in the headline "Lion on the Loose!" grabs the reader's attention and makes them want to read the article. Text A doesn't use language techniques in the same way because it is from a private diary that isn't intended to grab a reader's attention.

Pages 42-43 — Comparing Texts

1. **a)** You should have circled: to inform
   b) No
   Any sensible explanation, e.g. 'The Canterville Ghost' is a story which aims to entertain the reader rather than inform. This is shown by the use of imagery and emotive language.
2. Any sensible answer, e.g. The similes help the reader to better imagine the fear and anxiety that the characters in 'The Intruder' and the visitors to Muncaster Castle feel when they encounter the supernatural.
3. **a)** You should have ticked: sensory language
   b) Any sensible examples, e.g. In 'The Intruder', Bushra feels "a biting chill creep through her body". In 'Haunted Holidays', visitors to Muncaster Castle have felt "an inexplicable chill".
4. Any sensible answer, e.g. They are both mischievous. Tom the Fool plays "pranks that torment unsuspecting visitors". The Canterville ghost has frightened people "into hysterics" just by grinning at them and has "blown out" people's candles.
5. Any sensible answer, e.g. 'The Canterville Ghost' follows a typical story layout with the text separated into paragraphs. On the other hand, 'Haunted Holidays' includes common layout features of articles, such as a subheading and columns.
6. Any sensible similarity that is supported by evidence from the texts, e.g. Both Muncaster Castle and the mansion in 'The Intruder' are very old. 'Haunted Holidays' says that Muncaster Castle has been in the same family for "as many as 900 years". 'The Intruder' refers to the mansion as a "relic", which suggests it is very old.
7. **a)** Any sensible answer, e.g. arrogant
   b) Any sensible example, e.g. He boasts that he has had "a brilliant and uninterrupted career" as a ghost.
   c) Any sensible answer that compares the two characters, e.g. Unlike the Canterville ghost, the ghostly girl's character in 'The Intruder' is fearful and timid, shown when she stammers "P-p-please". However, neither character is malicious. The Canterville ghost enjoys scaring people but doesn't physically harm them, and the ghostly girl reassures Bushra that she means her "no harm".
8. Any sensible answer, e.g. There is an eerie mood in 'The Intruder'. The "cold stone walls" and "inky blackness" of the mansion create a dark atmosphere, and the "odd noises" in the mansion make it seem creepy. The mood of 'The Canterville Ghost' is also eerie at first, as the author describes the "ghastly green light" and the ghost's "hollow groans". However, the mood becomes gradually more lighthearted. The ghost's annoyance at not being able to frighten the occupants of the house creates humour for the reader, which lightens the mood.
9. Any two sensible paragraphs that compare the two texts, e.g.
   - In both texts, language is used to engage the reader. In 'Haunted Holidays', the author uses alliteration, such as "ghostly goings-on" and "creepily creaked open" to make the events reported in the article sound more interesting. In 'The Intruder', the author uses lots of imagery to bring Bushra's fear to life for the reader. For example, Bushra describes "Uneasiness" washing over her "like a stormy wave".
   - The tone of the texts is very different. In 'Haunted Holidays', the author includes lots of facts about the ghostly happenings at Muncaster Castle, and they offer their opinion on the events they are describing, using phrases such as "This is hardly surprising" and "It is somewhat unfair". This creates an informative and analytical tone. On the other hand, the tone of 'The Intruder' is eerie and sinister. The author uses sensory language such as "inky blackness" and "cold stone walls" to create a menacing mood for the reader.

Section 6: Reading Review

Page 45 — Reading Review

1. Any quote that suggests the farm is doing well, e.g. "the young wheat was thick and green" *[1 mark]*
2. Any sensible answer, e.g. "terror and slaughter" *[1 mark]*
3. Any sensible answer, e.g. She feels upset. *[1 mark]* The author describes how "her eyes filled with tears". *[1 mark]*
4. Any sensible answer, e.g. They wanted to overthrow the humans. *[1 mark]*
5. **a)** Any sensible summary, e.g. Clover hoped that the rebellion would lead to a peaceful society where all animals were free and equal *[1 mark]*, and where animals would look after one another. *[1 mark]*
   b) No, they have not achieved this outcome. *[1 mark]*
   Any two sensible reasons, e.g.
   The animals are not free and equal because they have to follow the orders of Napoleon. *[1 mark]*
   The strong do not protect the weak. Instead, "fierce, growling dogs" roam around intimidating weaker animals. *[1 mark]*
6. Any sensible answer, e.g. They stay silent because they are too scared to speak their minds. *[1 mark]* If they say what they think about the current situation, they risk being "torn to pieces" by dogs. *[1 mark]*

7   You should have used details from the text to describe Clover's change in attitude.
    1-2 marks for a simple answer that uses some evidence from the text to describe Clover's change in attitude.
    3-4 marks for a well-developed answer that is supported by details from the text to clearly describe Clover's change in attitude.
    Here are some points and evidence you may have included:
    - Clover supported the original rebellion, but she does not think it has achieved its aims. She thinks that the current situation is "not what they had looked forward to" when they rebelled.
    - She is upset that their dreams of freedom have led to fear and violence. She cries when she thinks about the "terror and slaughter" that they have seen.
    - Despite her concerns, she supports the current system because she thinks that the animals are "far better off" than when the humans were in control.

Page 47 — Reading Review

1   To discuss Martin's return to school *[1 mark]*
2   Any sensible answer, e.g. They should speak hesitantly. *[1 mark]* The dashes create pauses in the lines, suggesting that the tutor is struggling to find the right words. *[1 mark]*
3   (*opens door wide*) *[1 mark]*
4   Any sensible answer, e.g. He doesn't want to hide from people, because they need to get used to his disfigurement. *[1 mark]* He has to return to school at some point, so he might as well get it over with. *[1 mark]*
5   Any sensible answer, e.g. Anthony acts as a voice inside Present Martin's head that advises him what to do. *[1 mark]* Anthony's dialogue offers answers to Present Martin's fears about going back, showing the audience how Martin overcame his reservations. *[1 mark]*
6   Any sensible answer, e.g. They are worried about him returning to school. *[1 mark]* The tutor is concerned that it "may be hard" for Martin because the other students will treat him differently. *[1 mark]*
7   Any sensible answer, e.g. I think the author included Narrative Martin to help the audience understand what is going on inside Present Martin's head. *[1 mark]* For example, Narrative Martin reveals to the audience that Present Martin is "so tempted" to request the rest of the term off, which the audience wouldn't necessarily know from Present Martin's dialogue with his tutor. *[1 mark]*

8   You should have used details from the text to describe and explain the impression you get of Martin as a character in the extract.
    1-3 marks for a simple answer that uses some details from the text to explain your impression of Martin's character.
    4-6 marks for a well-developed answer that is supported by details from the text to clearly explain your impression of Martin's character.
    Here are some points and explanations you may have included:
    - Martin is brave because he decides to return to school even though he knows people "will stare".
    - He is proud because he refuses to "hide" and is "not ashamed" of his disfigurement.
    - He is stubborn because once he makes up his mind, he refuses to listen to his form tutor's protests.
    - He is logical because he carefully thinks through his options and reflects, thinking "What would Anthony do?".
    - He can be rude. He interrupts his form tutor several times.
    - He is appreciative because he thanks his form tutor for their thoughtfulness at the end of the extract.

Page 49 — Reading Review

1   They liked the cover of the book. *[1 mark]*
2   Any sensible summary, e.g. *Someone, No one* is about a teenage girl called Estaa who has magical powers. *[1 mark]* It takes place in a fantasy world where there are fairies, wizards and dragons. *[1 mark]*. The story is about Estaa growing up and taking on the challenges that an ordinary teenager faces, as well as some magical ones. *[1 mark]*
3   a) "I hunt my prey like a wolf" *[1 mark]*
    b) Any sensible explanation, e.g. To suggest that the writer really wants to read a new book *[1 mark]*. It suggests that the reader is a predator and the new book is their prey. *[1 mark]*
4   You should have given:
    Two layout features *[2 marks]*
    Explanations of the effect of each feature *[2 marks]*
    Here are some features and explanations you may have included:
    - Heading — This introduces the topic of the review clearly and captures the reader's attention.
    - Subheadings — These help to divide the text into manageable chunks, making it easier to read.
    - Columns — These are a common feature of newspaper articles and help make the text easy to read and fit better on the page.
    - Text box — This makes the information inside it stand out from the rest of the article.
    - Numbered list — This makes the writer's ranking of fantasy books clear.

5   a) To persuade the reader to read *Someone, No one*. *[1 mark]*
    b) Any sensible answer, e.g. The writer uses persuasive language techniques. *[1 mark]* They use a list of three to vividly describe the book as "beautiful, descriptive, gripping". *[1 mark]* The writer also uses a series of rhetorical questions, such as "Do you simply enjoy a good book?" to convince the reader that the novel will suit their taste in books. *[1 mark]*
6   Any sensible answer, e.g. The tone of the review is enthusiastic but analytical. *[1 mark]* The writer's enthusiasm encourages the reader to read *Someone, No one* and their analytical tone makes the reader respect their opinion. *[1 mark]*
7   You should have used details from the text to summarise and explain the author's opinion in the text.
    1-2 marks for a simple summary of the writer's opinion that is supported by some evidence from the text.
    3-4 marks for a detailed summary of the writer's opinion that is supported by evidence from throughout the text.
    Here are some points and evidence you may have included:
    - The writer really enjoyed *Someone, No one*. They liked its cover and said that the book itself was "as mysterious, interesting and beautiful" as the cover.
    - The writer particularly enjoyed the author's writing style, which they described as "brilliant" and "confident".
    - The writer doesn't normally like fantasy novels, so the fact that they were "captivated" by *Someone, No one* suggests that they thought it was very good.
    - The writer had a few criticisms of the book, for example they felt that some of the characters and parts of the plot could have been developed more.
8   Any sensible answer, e.g. Based on this review, I would like to read *Someone, No one*. *[1 mark]* The review makes the book sound like a really interesting read by describing it as "gripping" and "superbly readable". *[1 mark]*

Page 51 — Reading Review

1   It is around nine in the morning. *[1 mark]*
2   a) Any sensible answer, e.g. Romeo feels sad *[1 mark]* Any sensible quote, e.g. "Sad hours seem long." *[1 mark]*
    b) Any sensible answer, e.g. Romeo feels sad because the woman he loves does not return his feelings. *[1 mark]* He tells Benvolio that he is "Out of her favour". *[1 mark]*
3   a) oxymoron *[1 mark]*
    b) Any sensible answer, e.g. It suggests that love is confusing *[1 mark]* because this description uses a series of opposites to describe love, such as "sick" and "health". *[1 mark]*
4   Any sensible answer, e.g. Benvolio is upset to see Romeo suffering because of love. *[1 mark]* He tells Romeo that he is crying because of the misery Romeo feels as a result of his "heart's oppression". *[1 mark]*
5   Any sensible answer, e.g. Romeo is a sensitive and emotional person *[1 mark]*. This is shown in his outburst of emotion when he confides in Benvolio about his feelings. *[1 mark]*
6   You should have used details from the text to explain how Shakespeare shows that Romeo and Benvolio have a close relationship.
    1-2 marks for a simple answer that uses some evidence from the text to explain how their close relationship is shown.
    3-4 marks for a well-developed answer that is supported by details from the text to clearly explain how their close relationship is shown.
    Here are some points and evidence you may have included:
    - Romeo and Benvolio are cousins and close friends and address each other informally as "coz".
    - The characters openly discuss their emotions with each other which suggests they share a close emotional bond.
    - Benvolio feels such empathy at Romeo's circumstances that he becomes upset on his behalf, which shows that Romeo's sadness has a profound impact on him.
    - Romeo seeks advice from Benvolio about the sensitive topic of love, showing that he trusts Benvolio deeply.

Answers

Section 7: Writing — Non-Fiction Writing

Page 52 — Before you Start

1. i) 2
   ii) 1
   iii) 3
2. A — to inform
   B — to persuade
   C — to advise
   D — to argue
3. a) E.g. I am unable to attend the Christmas party.
   b) E.g. There are many fascinating artefacts in the museum.
   c) E.g. We must avoid that film — it is dreadful.

Page 53 — Planning

1. a) B is the better plan.
      Any sensible explanation, e.g. The layout in Plan B is easier to follow and it doesn't include irrelevant information.
   b) Any sensible plan that corrects the mistakes mentioned in part a).
2. a) Any sensible plan for one of the topics, e.g.
      Introduction — The school should donate to a local food bank.
      Point 1 — Schools should do their bit to help out people in the local community.
      Point 2 — Schools often end up with a lot of surplus food at the end of the week that would be wasted otherwise.
      Point 3 — Donating to food banks would set a good example to school pupils about the importance of contributing positively to society.
      Conclusion — The school needs to set up a scheme to donate to local food banks.
   b) Any sensible letter that follows the plan in part a).

Page 54-55 — Structure

1. Any sensible explanation, e.g. Introduction B is clearer and written in a more formal style, compared to Introduction A which is more informal and contains irrelevant information.
2. a) 1 — First and foremost...
      2 — However...
      3 — These physical and mental benefits...
   b) You should have ticked: ii)
   c) Any sensible conclusion to the text, e.g. The facts above demonstrate that yoga is suitable for and beneficial to everyone. Whether you are looking for a new way to get fit or a way to make friends, yoga may be the answer you've been looking for.
3. Many people wrongly assume that they can get away with not wearing suncream on cloudy days. However, evidence shows that a large percentage of the sun's damaging rays can penetrate clouds. This shows just how vital it is to protect your skin with suncream every day, regardless of the weather.
4. a) You should have ticked iii)
   b) Any sensible sentence that completes the paragraph e.g. Participants in these studies explained that they were able to work without distractions when they started early and could focus more easily on the job at hand.
5. Any sensible paragraph that has a clear structure, e.g. Dogs tend to make better pets than cats. Most dogs enjoy human company and are loyal to their family, whereas cats are known to display more independent behaviour and often visit multiple families for food. This proves that dogs are superior to cats because they are always there when you need them.
6. a) Any three points about your favourite hobby that will convince others to try it, e.g.
      1) The repetitiveness of cross-stitching is very therapeutic.
      2) A wide range of patterns are available for different abilities and interests.
      3) Finishing a project is extremely satisfying.
   b) Any sensible article that includes the points mentioned in part a), an engaging introduction and a clear conclusion.

Page 56 — Quoting

1. a) False
   b) False
   c) True
   d) True
2. B has used quotes incorrectly. There should be quotation marks either side of "a whirlpool" in the first sentence. Moreover, "strange powers" has been misquoted as "special powers".
3. Any sensible paragraph that weaves quotes b) and c) into the extract, e.g. The author describes the abandoned laboratory using sensory language. By referring to "the acrid smell of old experiments" and the feel of the "cobwebs" as they "tickled" the narrator's "legs", the author engages the reader's senses. This helps them to better imagine what the laboratory is like after being vacant for so long.

Page 57 — Writing Essays

1. Any sensible plans that include three main points for each essay, e.g.
   1) School holidays are for students to relax and take time out from their studies.
   2) Making students do homework during the holidays increases stress and reduces their free time.
   3) School work and students' personal time should be kept separate.

2 a) Any sensible question, e.g. Explain the advantages and disadvantages of using public transport.
   b) Any two sensible advantages, e.g. Fewer cars mean quieter and safer roads. Travelling by train is often quicker than travelling by car.
   c) Any two sensible disadvantages, e.g. People are restricted to travelling at times when buses and trains run, which can be inconvenient. Trains and buses can be too full for more passengers to get on.
   d) Any sensible summary of a suitable conclusion for the essay, e.g. Public transport needs many improvements to reach its potential.
   e) Any sensible essay that answers the question written in part a), includes all of the points in the plan and includes additional information from parts b) - d).

Page 58 — Formal and Informal Language

1 Any sensible examples of texts e.g.
   Informal:
   A diary entry about your holiday last year.
   An email to your friend about a trip to the zoo.
   A blog post about your favourite films.
   Formal:
   An essay that compares two poems.
   A letter requesting a refund for a faulty item.
   A speech about reducing litter.
2 a) E.g. She was disappointed that she was unable to meet her friend for a drink.
   b) E.g. I believe I am well suited to the job you have advertised on your website.
   c) E.g. We were famished so we purchased some refreshments.
3 Any sensible paragraph for a formal letter that uses all of the words in the box, e.g.
   I am writing to <u>enquire</u> whether I could have your <u>assistance</u> on a matter of <u>considerable</u> importance. It seems that all of my documents have the <u>incorrect</u> personal details on them. My <u>occupation</u> is a paramedic. <u>However</u>, on my account, it is listed as a parachutist. Could you help me <u>verify</u> my details so I can <u>demonstrate</u> that I am who I claim to be?
4 Any sensible letter that uses appropriate informal language.

Pages 59-60 — Writing to Inform, Explain and Advise

1 Uses examples and evidence to help someone understand — E
   Gives suggestions with polite language rather than commands — A
   Usually assumes the reader knows nothing about the topic — E
   Gives the reader lots of facts, presented in an engaging way — I
   Often addresses the reader with second-person pronouns — A
   Provides clear, balanced information about a certain topic — I

2 a) Any sensible answer, e.g. Eating fruit and vegetables like bananas and carrots provides us with the vitamins and minerals that we need for a healthy diet.
   b) Any sensible answer, e.g. Volunteers can support people who need it while learning a wide variety of skills, such as teamwork and problem solving.
   c) Any sensible answer, e.g. You may fall behind in your school work if you go on holiday during term time, because you might miss important lessons and have to take extra lessons to catch up.
3 Any sensible paragraph, e.g. Beetroots are incredible vegetables. They are packed full of vitamins and minerals, which means they are very good for you. Not only are they healthy, they are also naturally sweet. This makes them an ideal baking ingredient for people who are looking to reduce their sugar intake. In addition to this, their potent pink juice can be used as a natural dye, which prevents the use of artificial colours in foods.
4 a) Any sensible answer, e.g. The text is telling people what to do rather than giving them polite suggestions.
   b) Any sensible text that gives polite suggestions, e.g. It is recommended to stay away from the beach when it is rainy or windy. You could stay inside and wait for the weather to improve instead. However, if you do need to go outside, you may find it useful to wear your waterproofs and wellies so you don't get soaked.
5 a) i) Any sensible sentences that give facts about your hometown and the surrounding area.
      ii) Any sensible sentences that give suggestions about the best things to do in your hometown.
   b) Any sensible article that explains how you feel about your hometown and includes the details mentioned in i) to iii).

Pages 61-62 — Writing to Persuade and Argue

1 a) False
   b) True
   c) True
2 Any sensible answers, e.g.
   a) I was horrified, disgusted and angry at the state of the hotel room.
   b) It is shameful, disheartening and unacceptable that we were treated in this way.
   c) This role would suit a hard-working, organised and confident individual like me.
3 "I think we can all agree..." — D
   "Some believe that the long break is beneficial..." — E
   "Why should we spend a whole year..." — A
   "I become bored, frustrated and lonely..." — C
   "I'm sure millions of students..." — B

4		Any sensible text that is more exaggerated, e.g. We're sure that you'll absolutely adore our resort. We have the best facilities in the world. Our famous swimming pool is still in perfect condition and our customers can't stop raving about our food. There's no doubt that you'll have a wonderful holiday if you stay with us this summer. We'll see you soon!
5	a)	You should have ticked: All types of pollution negatively impact our fragile planet. Any sensible explanation, e.g. It uses strong language like "negatively impact" to make its argument more effective, whereas the other sentences use words that suggest uncertainty, like "might" and "probably".
	b)	Any sensible changes, e.g. Signing a petition <u>will</u> make <u>no difference whatsoever</u>. <u>It is essential</u> that robots be used to do household chores.
6	a)	Any sensible paragraph that argues in favour of the idea that no student should get away with bullying others.
	b)	Any sensible paragraph that argues in favour of the idea that people deserve more time to do the things they enjoy.
7	a)	Persuasive writing should not directly <u>attack</u> your opponents. Instead, any <u>criticisms</u> should be <u>impersonal</u> and general. However, you should refer to "we" or "you" when making <u>positive</u> points, as this will help to <u>involve</u> the reader and encourage them to <u>support</u> you.
	b)	Any sensible changes to the text that make the criticisms general and the positive points personal, e.g. Anyone who thinks this problem doesn't concern them is a fool. It is cruel to sit idly and let people suffer — ignoring a problem does not make it go away. We must unite to solve this problem with our compassion. Only then can we triumph over ignorance.

Section 8: Writing — Fiction Writing

Page 63 — Before you Start

1		You should have ticked: a), c) and e)
2		A — horror B — science fiction C — fairy tale
3	a)	Any sensible answer, e.g. He pressed his back flat against the wall and cautiously looked around the corner.
	b)	Any sensible answer, e.g. She flopped down at her desk and sighed as she typed out yet another letter.

Page 64 — Planning

1		You should have ticked: c)
2	a)	Any sensible answer, e.g. The plan doesn't give a clear structure for the story and it suggests multiple possible plot lines.
	b)	Any two sensible suggestions, e.g. The plot points could be written in the order that they will happen in the story. The plan could give only one developed plot line.
	c)	Any sensible plan that includes the changes suggested in part b).
3		Any sensible opening sentence, plot points and ending that fit in with the rest of the plan.

Page 65 — Structure

1	a)	You should have ticked: A part of a story that takes the reader back to past events.
	b)	Any sensible answer, e.g. The narrative could include a flashback to a mysterious event in the main character's past that makes the reader see the character and the present day narrative differently.
2	a)	1 — A family are on holiday on a tropical island. 2 — While they are out sailing... 3 — In an attempt to steer away from the storm... 4 — The family wash up on shore... 5 — During their stay...
	b)	Any three sensible plot points that fit with the rest of the story and develop the plot in an exciting way.

Page 66 — Building Character

1	a)	Any sensible answer, e.g. It suggests that Natalie might be unkind because she seems to enjoy the idea of hitting her brother with the ball.
	b)	Any sensible answer, e.g. It suggests that Raheem is a nice person to be around.
2	a)	You should have underlined: Unless your dilemma involved animals, in which case she'd ignore you completely.
	b)	Any sensible answer, e.g. Laura is presented as a kind and caring person, which is not reflected in this sentence.
	c)	Any sensible sentence, e.g. If your dilemma involved animals, she would want to know all about how she could help.

3   Any sensible paragraphs where both actions and appearance are used to describe the characters in the pictures, e.g.
    A — The door crashed open and the sound of heavy footsteps grew louder. The employees ducked behind their computer screens to avoid meeting Mr Lewis's icy glare.
    B — In two powerful strides, she reached the edge of the gorge and leapt across, her strong leg muscles flexing. She landed with a skid, heart racing, and grinned.
    C — Petra's eyes were wide as she tucked herself behind the door. She gripped the door handle tightly, ready to slam it shut if the terrifying kitten took another paw-step closer.
    D — With his jaw clenched and beads of sweat on his forehead, Jeffrey sat down in front of the crowd. As he prepared to play the first note, a phone rang in the audience. Unable to control his frustration, he let out a strangled screech.

Page 67 — Building Setting

1   a) Any sensible description, e.g.
       The imposing trees loomed over the rest of the forest and prevented the light from reaching the forest floor. The narrow path snaked its way into the bowels of the forest, eventually widening into an unnatural clearing that was guarded by an abandoned shack.
    b) Any sensible description, e.g.
       The majestic trunks stretched high into the air, shading us from the intense sun overhead. The paved path guided us deeper into the lush greenery, eventually widening to reveal a tranquil clearing. At the edge of the clearing stood a quaint cottage.
2   Any sensible paragraphs which describe the setting and create the desired atmosphere.
3   a) Any sensible answer, e.g. The start of the story should have a troubled atmosphere to show the colony's worry.
    b) Any sensible answer, e.g. The setting descriptions should make Antarctica seem almost alien. There could also be comparisons to snowier and happier times to highlight how much Antarctica has suffered since the snow started melting.
    c) Any sensible setting description that uses the answers from parts a) and b), e.g. Everything looked different. Where once there was a landscape of ice as clear as glass, there was now only dry dust. The blanket of snow that normally made everything look so clean and comforting was nowhere to be seen. The harsh sun continued to beat down on the continent without faltering. Something had to change.

Page 68 — Writing Stories

1   Any sensible opening sentences, e.g.
    a) We used to think time travel was a load of nonsense, but that was before we found the machine...
    b) Whenever Carys's friends were asked to describe her, they'd all say she was ordinary.
    c) It was the early hours of the morning and Dr Staples was still working tirelessly in his lab.
    d) I stirred, suddenly aware of strange noises coming from outside my bedroom window.
2   a) Any sensible answer that states a suitable atmosphere for the story and explains what can be done to create it.
    b) Any sensible description of two main characters in the story that includes the information mentioned in the bullet points.
    c) Any sensible plan that uses the details in the relevant summary.
    d) Any sensible story that covers all the points included in the plan in part c) as well as the atmosphere mentioned in part a) and the character descriptions in part b).

Page 69 — Writing Scripts

1   Any sensible stage directions that show the actors what to do and how to speak, e.g.
    LEAH: [whispering] Pssst! Akio? Are you there? I've found firewood.
    [AKIO jumps out from behind a rock]
    LEAH: [loud and angry] Hey! You made me drop all the wood!
    AKIO: [putting his finger to his lips] Shhh! You're going to lead the dragon right to us!
    LEAH: Don't jump out at me then! Now help me start this fire. It's a blizzard out there.
    AKIO: [rolling his eyes] How is lighting a beacon for the dragon going to help Tim?
    LEAH: [abruptly] Well I doubt freezing to death is going to help him either.
    [pauses] I'm sorry... I didn't mean to snap. I'm just scared for Tim.
    AKIO: [taking Leah's hand] We won't let anything bad happen to him. I promise.
2   a) Any sensible answer that describes how the characters would be feeling.
    b) Any sensible answer that describes how the characters would speak and behave.
    c) Any sensible script for A, B or C that includes the points mentioned in i) to iii).

Page 70 — Poetry

1   a)   Free verse
         Any sensible explanation, e.g. The poem doesn't have a regular rhythm or rhyme scheme.
    b)   Any sensible examples, e.g.
         hearing — carol singers
         touch — cold breeze
         smell — smoke from chimneys
         taste — mince pies
         sight — white snow
    c)   Any five-line stanza that describes a sense per line. The lines don't have to rhyme.
2   a)   Any sensible answer that states a tone and explains how it can be achieved.
    b)   Any sensible answer that describes how the reader should feel when they read the poem.
    c)   Any sensible poem that has the tone mentioned in part a), creates the desired effect from part b), and follows the checklist in part c).

Section 9: Writing — Writing Properly

Page 71 — Before you Start

1   You should have ticked: a), c), d), f) and h)
2   a)   <u>Its</u> my birthday tomorrow and I'm finally going to be thirteen <u>year's</u> old. My birthday is at the start of August so all of my <u>friend's</u> birthdays are before mine. At least I <u>dont</u> have to go to school on my birthday though. When the <u>weathers</u> nice, we usually host a family barbecue at my <u>grandmas'</u> house because her garden is huge. She also makes the best birthday <u>cake's</u>, but it's a secret recipe.
    b)   It's, years, friends', don't, weather's, grandma's, cakes
3   a)   I <u>believe</u> I should <u>practise</u> the guitar more often.
    b)   The book's main <u>character</u> is really <u>fascinating</u>.
    c)   My doctor <u>referred</u> me to the hospital for <u>treatment</u>.

Page 72 — Punctuation Mix

1   a)   You need to buy these things at the shop<u>:</u> onions, milk and cheese.
    b)   We can't go camping until tomorrow<u>:</u> it's supposed to rain today.
    c)   Elijah and Beatrice were late for school<u>:</u> they couldn't find their shoes.
    d)   I'm so nervous<u>:</u> I have a dance recital in the morning.
2   a)   Wilfred Owen (an English poet) fought in the First World War.
    b)   My cousin is getting married in the summer (21st August).
    c)   The National Equine Institute for Giant Horses (NEIGH) is closed.

3   a)   Delilah played golf at the weekend; Ikenna went to a restaurant with his friends.
    b)   I wake up early to go for a run; my sister stays in bed until eleven o'clock.
    c)   Audrey has had a productive day: she finished the book that she only started yesterday; baked a cake (a lemon one) for dessert; and tidied all of the mess on her bedroom floor.
4   Any sensible rewriting of the story that uses direct speech correctly, e.g.
         "Mum!" shouted Martha. "Have you seen my skateboard?"
         "Have you checked under your bed?" replied Mum. "That's where I last saw it."
         Martha looked under her bed. "It's not there either," she called.
         "WHEEEEEEE!" squealed a voice outside. Her younger sister had taken her skateboard without asking.
         "Get off my skateboard!" Martha bellowed at her sister. "You're going to break it!"

Page 73 — Structuring Your Writing

1   A — Hail assailed the windows while Clara listened intently to her uncle's spooky story. She clutched her cushion for comfort. <u>//</u> "Those who drift too close to the haunted cliffs never return..." he whispered, as if he feared the cliffs themselves might hear him.
         A new person is speaking.
         B — Before we begin, I want to thank you all for attending this gala. The money you have raised will greatly support the animals in our shelter. <u>//</u> I founded this charity ten years ago with one goal: to help as many animals as I could.
         A new time is mentioned.
         C — In the future, I would love to visit Machu Picchu. The history of the Inca Empire has always fascinated me and the photos look spectacular. To get there, you can take a train or hike from the city of Cuzco. <u>//</u> I also want to visit Italy because I love pizza.
         A new point is being made.
2   The personification of the forest shows that the author believes that the forest is sentient, highlighting their deep connection with the place in which they grew up.
         <u>Additionally</u>, the use of onomatopoeia lets the reader form their own connection to the forest as they can easily imagine its sounds, as if they were there too.
         <u>On the one hand</u>, both of these techniques could have been used to simply help the reader better understand the importance of the forest to the author.
         <u>Alternatively</u>, the author may have built this connection so that the forest's destruction is more tragic to the reader, allowing them to better understand the author's pain.

3   Any essay that includes an introduction, a paragraph for each of the points made in the plan, and a conclusion, and uses sensible linking words to help the paragraphs flow smoothly.

Page 74 — Redrafting and Proofreading

1 a) You should have ticked the final paragraph.
   b) Any sensible explanation, e.g. The writer has used short, simple sentences which don't flow as well as the other two paragraphs.
   c) Any sensible paragraph that solves the problems mentioned in part b), e.g.
      The police have requested that any witnesses contact them and make a statement about what they have seen. They are especially interested in information regarding the identity of the robbers. They have also asked people to come forward if they have recently had a black van stolen from the local area.

2 My energy reserves <u>where</u> (were) fading as day became night. Luckily, the lighthouse <u>iluminated</u> (illuminated) the path, <u>it's</u> (its) pulsing light guiding me through the shadows until <u>Id</u> (I'd) almost reached home. Suddenly, a loud bang startled me, and I was <u>plundged</u> (plunged) into darkness. The <u>opressive</u> (oppressive) shadows swallowed my feet and I couldn't see the next step. I took a deep breath: <u>may be</u> (maybe) everything would be fine if I could make it <u>too</u> (to) the bridge near my house. I stumbled to where the old <u>whethered</u> (weathered) posts ought to be and gingerly felt for the first plank. However<u>_</u> (,) I found something scarier<u>;</u> (—)absolutely nothing<u>_</u> (.).

Section 10: Writing — Making It Interesting

Page 75 — Before you Start

1   Any sensible answers, e.g.
  a) The weather was <u>glorious</u> so I <u>strolled</u> through the park.
  b) Robin <u>investigated</u> the <u>mysterious</u> noise in the attic.

2 a) onomatopoeia
   b) metaphor
   c) simile
   d) exaggeration (hyperbole)
   e) personification

3 a) A — iii)
      B — i)
      C — ii)

   b) Any sensible answers, e.g.
      A — I got to the cinema and bought some popcorn. Then, I sat down and waited for the film to start.
      B — Manuel was upset about how late his lunch had arrived.
      C — It was unkind of those children to play a nasty prank on Beth. She wasn't even mean to them.

Page 76 — Using Different Techniques

1 a) You should have ticked: i) and ii)
   b) Any sensible answers, e.g.
      iii) Last summer was hotter than the surface of the sun.
      iv) Alice was happier than a mouse in a cheese factory.

2 a) Any sensible explanation, e.g.
      Text A uses very long sentences which need to be broken up. Text B uses very short sentences which could be combined. Both texts could also use more interesting vocabulary.
   b) Any sensible answer, e.g.
      Thunder rumbled loudly outside. I'm terrified of thunder so I darted upstairs to the safety of my bed. Minutes later, there was an even closer rumble of thunder. Hiding under the covers, I tried to push the incessant noise from my mind. I hoped it would end soon.

3 Any sensible answer, e.g.
   Last weekend, he went to the zoo. As soon as he arrived, he bought a map and some feed for the goats in the petting zoo. Out of all of the animals, the apes were his favourite, especially the baby gorilla. He thought the snakes were quite scary though. At lunchtime, he bought a hot dog and a magnet for his fridge as a souvenir.

Page 77 — Figurative Language

1   Any sensible answers, e.g.
  a) The crowd was a clan of hysterical hyenas.
  b) Farah's eyes are glittering emeralds.
  c) The fridge was a barren wasteland.

2   Any three sensible similes, e.g. Students waiting at the bus stop huddle like penguins.

3 a) Any sensible answer, e.g. Its familiar pages welcomed me back gladly.
   b) Any sensible answer, e.g. The old train rattled and clanked as it made its way through the landscape.
   c) Any sensible answer, e.g. I was so nervous that I thought my heart would leap out of my chest.

Section 11: Writing Review

Pages 78-79 — Writing Review

1 a) You should have ticked: to entertain *[1 mark]*
   b) Any sensible answer, e.g. Include lots of interesting language and an exciting plot to keep the reader engaged. *[1 mark]*

2 a) teenagers *[1 mark]*
   b) Any sensible answer, e.g. Include a relatable character so that they connect to the story. *[1 mark]*

3 a) Any sensible setting, e.g.
       a mountain range *[1 mark]*
       Any sensible explanation, e.g. The aim of the campaign is to encourage teenagers to explore nature, so an outdoor setting like this would be appropriate. *[1 mark]*
   b) Any three sensible sentences that describe the chosen setting e.g.
       The powdery snow sparkled like diamonds in the morning sun. *[1 mark]* This pure white blanket contrasted starkly with the tall, granite spires of rock that reached into the clouds. *[1 mark]* Protected by their thick, cloudy shields, the distant summit of each mountain was shrouded from view. *[1 mark]*

4 a) Any three sensible traits, e.g.
       considerate, athletic, outdoorsy *[1 mark]*
   b) Any sensible answers, e.g.
       If she comes across fallen branches on the mountain trail, she could move them out of the way so that other hikers won't trip. *[1 mark]*
       Every weekend, she could wake up early and run up the mountain. *[1 mark]*
       She could spend her free time high up in the mountains, away from the sound of traffic and tourists. *[1 mark]*
   c) Any sensible answers, e.g.
       She could have strong legs because she is very athletic. *[1 mark]*.
       She could wear walking boots because she spends a lot of time hiking outdoors. *[1 mark]*

5 Any sensible plan, e.g.
   Engaging opening — Main character is at the top of a mountain observing the beauty of the area where they live. *[1 mark]*
   Plot development 1 — Main character discovers that a mining company want to mine for minerals in the mountain. *[1 mark]*
   Plot development 2 — Main character has to prove the mountain is worth preserving. *[1 mark]*
   Plot development 3 — She finds a network of caves full of rare wildlife. *[1 mark]*
   Satisfying ending — The mountain is granted protected status so has to be preserved. *[1 mark]*

6 Any two sensible ways, e.g.
   The story could begin with a flashforward that shows the main character in danger while protecting the mountain. *[1 mark]*
   The story could include short chapters that end on cliffhangers. *[1 mark]*

7 Use the information below to help you mark your story.
   Your story should include: a detailed description of the setting *[1 mark]*, a plot development that threatens the setting *[1 mark]*, and a strategy for saving the setting in the story *[1 mark]*.
   Your story should be suitable for teenagers *[1 mark]* and it should be entertaining *[1 mark]* and positive about nature *[1 mark]*. It should also include interesting vocabulary *[1 mark]* and a range of sentence structures *[1 mark]*. The spelling, punctuation and grammar should be accurate (if you've made some mistakes, give yourself 1 mark) *[2 marks]*.

Page 80 — Writing Review

1 Any sensible answer, e.g. The tone should be formal and respectful because it will be read by the headteacher *[1 mark]*, but it should also be critical as it is arguing against their report. *[1 mark]*

2 Any three sensible arguments against what your headteacher has said, e.g.
   Languages are becoming increasingly important as the world becomes more connected. *[1 mark]*
   There are many professions where knowledge of languages is more valuable than extensive knowledge of core subjects. *[1 mark]*
   Removing languages from the curriculum could restrict the career prospects of students. *[1 mark]*
   Any sensible plan that outlines an engaging introduction *[1 mark]*, at least three sensible arguments *[1 mark]*, and a convincing conclusion *[1 mark]*.

3 Any sensible answer that includes an argument from Question 2 that has been expanded with more detail, e.g.
   Removing languages from the curriculum could restrict students' careers. There are many professions, like translation and international relations, where knowledge of languages is more valuable than extensive knowledge of core subjects. *[1 mark]*
   This suggests that, while more practice in English, maths and science is useful, future career choices could be restricted if pupils do not have knowledge of a language. *[1 mark]*

4 Any sensible counter arguments, e.g.
   You said in your report that you believe English, maths and science are more important to students' post-16 careers *[1 mark]*. While I do not disagree that these subjects are important, foreign language skills are increasingly demanded by employers because more and more foreign countries are working together. By cutting languages provision at our school, our careers are being hindered instead of helped. *[1 mark]*

5 Use the information below to help you mark your letter.

Your letter should include at least three arguments about why languages should still be taught in your school *[3 marks]*, and information about how studying languages is beneficial to students. *[1 mark]*

Your letter should be aimed at the headteacher of your school *[1 mark]*, and it should have a formal tone *[1 mark]*. It should also include interesting vocabulary *[1 mark]* and a range of sentence structures *[1 mark]*. The spelling, punctuation and grammar should be accurate (if you've made some mistakes, give yourself 1 mark) *[2 marks]*

Page 81 — Writing Review

Use the information below to help you mark your writing tasks.

Task 1 Your fairy tale should include: a detailed description of the setting *[1 mark]*, detailed descriptions of both a hero and a villain *[2 marks]*, and a conflict that takes place between the hero and the villain *[1 mark]*. Your fairy tale should be suitable for people attending a Literary Festival *[1 mark]* and it should be entertaining *[1 mark]*. It should also include interesting vocabulary *[1 mark]* and a range of sentence structures *[1 mark]*. The spelling, punctuation and grammar should be accurate (if you've made some mistakes, give yourself 1 mark) *[2 marks]*.

Task 2 Your leaflet should include: explanations of why exercising and eating a balanced diet are important *[2 marks]*, suggestions for healthier alternatives to unhealthy foods *[1 mark]* and suggestions for ways to integrate exercise into a daily routine *[1 mark]*.

Your leaflet should be aimed at the customers of your local supermarket *[1 mark]* and it should advise the reader *[1 mark]*. It should also include interesting vocabulary *[1 mark]* and a range of sentence structures *[1 mark]*. The spelling, punctuation and grammar should be accurate (if you've made some mistakes, give yourself 1 mark) *[2 marks]*.

Task 3 Your script should include: at least two teenage characters with different opinions about social media not working *[2 marks]*, helpful and clear stage directions *[1 mark]*, an appropriate resolution to the story *[1 mark]*.

Your script should be suitable for all ages *[1 mark]* and it should be entertaining *[1 mark]*. It should also include interesting vocabulary *[1 mark]* and a range of sentence structures *[1 mark]*. The spelling, punctuation and grammar should be accurate (if you've made some mistakes, give yourself 1 mark) *[2 marks]*.

Task 4 Your essay should include: a description of the place that you are suggesting *[1 mark]*, reasons why you think it would be a suitable place for a school trip *[2 marks]*, evidence that supports the reasons that you have given *[1 mark]*.

Your essay should be aimed at your teachers *[1 mark]* and it should have a formal tone *[1 mark]*. It should also include interesting vocabulary *[1 mark]* and a range of sentence structures *[1 mark]*. The spelling, punctuation and grammar should be accurate (if you've made some mistakes, give yourself 1 mark) *[2 marks]*.

Answers